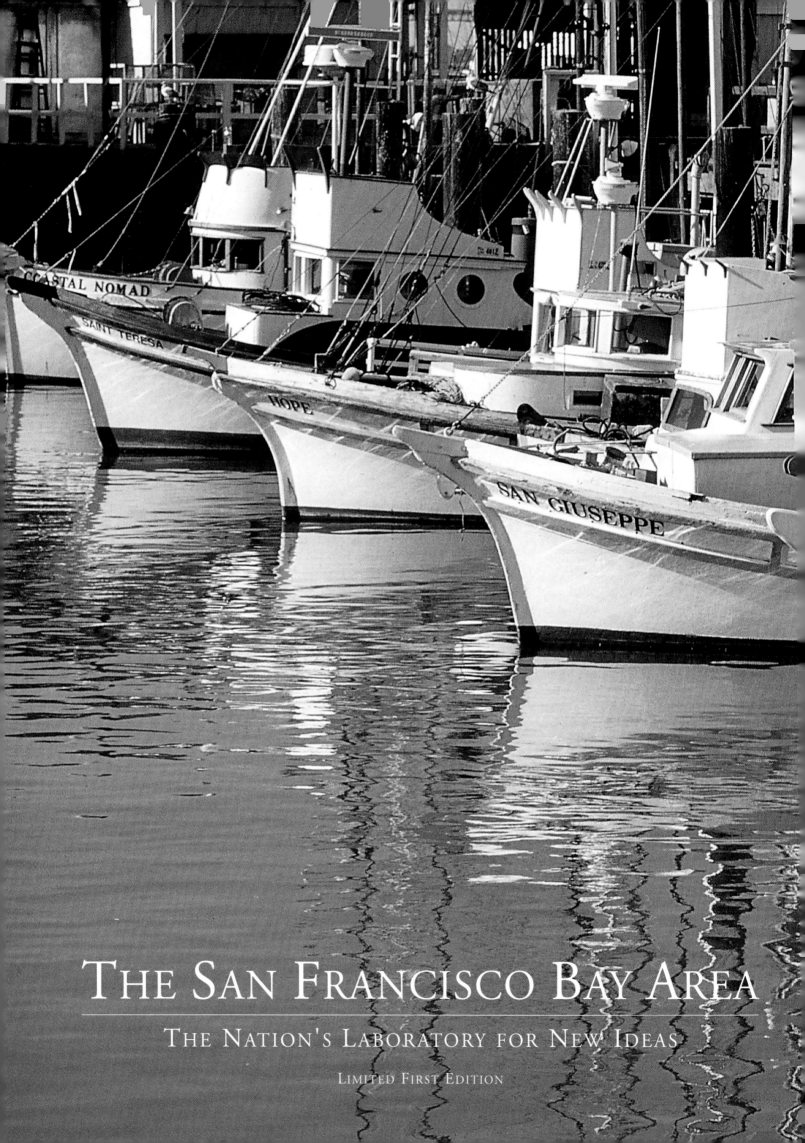

THE SAN FRANCISCO BAY AREA

THE NATION'S LABORATORY FOR NEW IDEAS

LIMITED FIRST EDITION

The publisher thanks the Mayor's Office of San Francisco for its sponsorship of this publication. Specifically, the publisher thanks Mayor Willie Brown and David Serrano-Sewell.

The publisher also wishes to thank the staff of the San Francisco Redevelopment Agency for its support and aid in the implementation of this project. In particular, the publisher thanks Clifford Graves, Kent Sims, Eila Arbuckle and Gwen Sebay. The publisher gratefully acknowledges the efforts and contributions made in the preparation of this publication by the San Francisco Convention and Visitors Bureau, the San Francisco Art Institute and the innumerable other groups and individuals whose help, cooperation and guidance made this project possible.

𝔚𝔓

Copyright 1997 by Wyndham Publications, Incorporated
Printed in the United States of America.

Library of Congress Catalog Card Number: 97-060057
Library of Congress Information:
    San Francisco Bay Area: The Nation's Laboratory for New Ideas
    Author: Corinne Murray

Contributing Writer & Biography Writer: Kathryn L. Supinski
Biography Writers: Kathryn Chetkovich, Lewis Wallace, Ruth Flaxman
Editor: Nancy Leichner
Design: Paul Langland Design
Illustrator: Steven Schildbach
Proofreaders: Kim Kubie and Corinne Murray

First Edition
Includes Bibliography, Index
ISBN: 0-9634100-4-0

Victorian doorway with flowers.

Bay Area color.

The Golden Gate Bridge snuggles under a fleecy blanket of fog as day breaks over San Francisco. The Bay Bridge and Telegraph Hill are visible at left.

San Francisco Convention & Visitors Bureau;
Photographer-Carl Wilmington

Chapter One

MORE THAN JUST A PRETTY FACE

More Than Just A Pretty Face

San Francisco.

It is a name that evokes images of scenic beauty, a rich and exciting history, cosmopolitan charm and cultural sophistication — a name that breathes the very spirit of romance. Its people simply call it The City, and it's not hard to see why.

But there is a lot more to The City, and to the surrounding communities, than just a place to leave your heart. As this book will demonstrate, the significance of the Bay Area on the worldwide stage rests on the area's longtime leadership in the fields of science, industry, and even social policy.

Many of the seminal inventions and events of the twentieth century were born here — from the splitting of the atom and creation of the microprocessor to the invention of television and the discovery of recombinant DNA. The innovative thinking and creative drive of its inhabitants through the past two centuries has helped the Bay Area exert a profound influence on business, science, the arts, and lifestyles around the world.

The San Francisco Bay Area is home to six million people — people who tend to be younger, wealthier, and better-educated than the average American. The area encompasses more than 100 political subdivisions, and reflects a rich variety of backgrounds, cultural traditions, values, and ethnic origins. Although San Francisco itself is one of the most densely-populated and developed cities in the U.S., it still has more acres of parkland per resident than any other major metropolis in the country. Its strategic mid-state location on the west coast makes it the northern center of California's vibrant economy, as well as the administrative center of the most productive agricultural region on earth, and the geographic hub of one of the world's fastest-growing economies. San Francisco is also one of the pivotal cities among Pacific Rim nations.

In little more than a generation, the world's economy has changed radically — and the rate of change will continue to quicken in generations to come. Today, virtually all business must compete in a global marketplace in which natural resources are no longer the major key to wealth, and geographical boundaries have little to do with economic

Bear Valley Station.

The old residences which gaze gothically over Alamo Square in San Francisco appear to have turned their backs on the 20th century with Victorian disapproval. The highest rises on the downtown skyline are the Transamerica Pyramid and the dark-hued Bank of America World Headquarters.

The sun silhouettes a cable car and a homebound San Franciscan on the crest of Russian Hill as fog drifts over the bay below.

activity. The ability to innovate, a broad data base, a well-managed information flow, and a highly-educated population, are the primary sources of modern economic strength — and it is in precisely these fields that the San Francisco Bay Area excels, thanks to the investment that has been made in the people and the infrastructure necessary to drive the business of today.

Education is definitely the foundation of the Bay Area economy. Nearly eight percent of the population is enrolled at the area's four world-class universities and 70 other accredited institutions of higher learning, where more than 17 percent of the local labor force is employed. The universities, laboratories, and libraries that thrive here serve as "factories" for new ideas, as do the arts groups and social movements for which the area is so well known. The curious, the questioning, and the creative find support and encouragement here, helping to make the Bay Area the world's most productive center for research and innovation.

That support and encouragement is rooted in the long-standing traditions of acceptance, tolerance, and experimentation which have produced unique social and political dynamics here. Anything can happen in San Francisco — and often has — because it has always been a city where unlimited possibilities await those who have the courage to seek them out. New scientific and sociological theories; new art forms, political movements, and lifestyles; all have been embraced by this very special city, along with ethnic diversity and even downright eccentricity. In San Francisco, to be "different" is still a very positive thing — as long as that difference comes with a personal vision of its own for tomorrow.

Deep-rooted traditions, a diverse cultural backdrop, a dynamic economy, beauty, charm, and hope: these are the things that make the San Francisco Bay Area one of the world's most favored places to live, to work, to raise a family, and to build a future.

All this, and cable-cars, too.

MEET ME AT THE FAIR

San Francisco began hosting large expositions with the Panama-Pacific International Exposition of 1915. Next came the Golden Gate International Exposition in 1939, for which space was made by the construction of the artificial Treasure Island, off Yerba Buena island in the Bay. Treasure Island was later taken over by the U.S. Navy, which is presently planning to turn it back over for private use. But The City's flair for fairs and festivals is not just at the international level. From impromptu block parties and neighborhood street fairs to citywide celebrations and nearby County Fairs, festivities go on all year 'round, much to the delight of all those who live or visit here.

Their catches landed, the boats of San Francisco's fishing fleet slumber in their berths at Fisherman's Wharf. Many of the Wharf's restaurants overlook the mooring basins.

A full moon and candle-like Coit Tower illuminate the multi-layered dwellings of San Francisco's Telegraph Hill.

San Francisco Convention & Visitors Bureau;
Photographer-Borje Svensson

An Economy Of New Ideas

Today's businesses and households alike are affected more profoundly by ideas, processes, and products developed in the Bay Area than most of us would ever guess. When you click on the *TV* to watch a *satellite* broadcast, put on your *permanent-press clothes*, take your *vitamins B and E*, or turn on your *personal computer* and *laserjet printer*, you are making daily use of Bay Area genius.

People in less prosperous places profit, too. Bay Area science has given birth to disease-fighting drugs and vaccines, as well as ways to increase crop yields. It is this widespread influence which makes the San Francisco Bay Area not only the nation's laboratory for new ideas, but the world's as well.

For more than 200 years, since its founding in 1776, San Francisco has attracted people of fertile imagination and strong personality — people who have created many of the most important, and well-known, products and technologies of the modern world. From Levi Strauss (1830-1902) and his "blue jeans" to Philo Farnsworth (1906-71) and his 1927 image dissector tube, which would later make television possible, these were individuals whose ideas and inventions would grow and thrive in the richly creative surroundings of the Bay Area. Their ranks also include:

David Peebles (1885-1965) who started out as an aspiring opera singer at the turn of the century, but soon became a power in the dairy industry. At the time of his death, he held some 70 patents, including one for the world's first true "instant food" — powdered milk.

Henry J. Kaiser (1882-1976), who built his Oakland-based empire from scratch, having dropped out of school at the age of 12. For 55 years, Kaiser Enterprises helped to build the country's great dams (Hoover, Bonneville, and Grand Coulee), launched over a quarter of the ships making up America's World War Two navy, and founded the nation's first and largest Health Maintenance Organization: Kaiser Permanente.

Glenn Salva, General Manager, and John Falcone, winemaker, taste the wares of Atlas Peak Vineyards in Napa Valley. Here, 35,000 square feet of wine aging caves are tunneled from the volcanic cliffs surrounding the property.

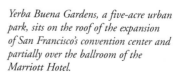

Yerba Buena Gardens, a five-acre urban park, sits on the roof of the expansion of San Francisco's convention center and partially over the ballroom of the Marriott Hotel.

PCL Construction

Perhaps best-known to the public at large is Santa Rosa resident Luther Burbank (1849-1926), who spent half a century breeding, hybridizing, and cultivating new species of vegetables, fruits, and flowers. Intrigued by the possibilities suggested by Darwin's theory of evolution, Burbank created more than 40 new plums and prunes, ten new berries, new breeds of tomatoes, corn, and peas — and, of course, new varieties of roses, lilies, poppies, and other flowers, including the ever-popular Shasta Daisy.

Contemporary innovators and entrepreneurs abound as well. Here Charles Schwab built the first, and by far the largest, discount brokerage house in the country. Today, a nationwide network of 110 branches serves 1.3 million customers holding equity of more than $25 billion in their accounts.

Some of the key insights of 20th-century science were born here. Sitting in a deli and scribbling down their ideas on a paper napkin, Herbert Boyer of the University of California, San Francisco, and Stanford's Stanley Cohen conceived experiments involving the transfer of genes from one organism to another — paving the way for molecular scientists who, in 1974, would use those concepts to create recombinant DNA, launching genetic engineering and the birth of the biotechnology industry.

Wine-making has always been important to northern California. One of the industry's major innovators is Robert Mondavi, who introduced such concepts as rotating fermentation tanks to extract more flavor and aroma, and varied fermentation temperatures to enhance specific flavors. He also developed a dry fermentation process to impart a dry flint taste to wines like Mondavi Fume Blanc. Today, Robert Mondavi Winery is a leading producer of premium California vintages.

Steven Jobs could well be described as the quintessential entrepreneur. In just five years, he took Apple Computer from a garage to the Fortune 500. Jobs, who is now Chairman and CEO of NeXT, Inc., believes that a company's work environment is as important to its success as its products.

The local creative community boasts such long-standing talents as Hal Riney, whose career has spanned more than four decades as a writer, art director, film producer, and entrepreneur, and who is responsible for some of the country's most memorable and enduring advertising.

Then there is the creator of *Star Wars* and *Indiana Jones*, film producer George Lucas, who has earned a reputation as a modern mythologist through his pioneering work with Marin County-based Lucasfilms, and the special-effects wonders created by Industrial Light & Magic.

Women have played a major role in San Francisco history, too. Julia Morgan (1872-1957), who was born in the city, is the most influential woman in the history of American architecture. The first female to graduate with a degree in mechanical engineering from the University of California, she was also the first woman graduate of the noted *Ecole des Beaux-Arts* in Paris. In a distinguished career spanning half a century, Morgan designed scores of public buildings and more than 600 private residences. In the first group are such monuments to her genius as the environmentally-sensitive Asilomar Conference Center at Pacific Grove. The most famous of the latter is undoubtedly the legendary Hearst Castle at San Simeon. San Francisco's Fairmont Hotel had its steel structure restored by Morgan after the 1906 earthquake and fire.

These Chardonnay grapes are ripening in the remarkable Alexander Valley vineyard of the Clos du Bois winery, whose distinctive wines have earned an enviable reputation for quality.

The Wine Alliance

Atlas Peak provides the background to the vineyards that are its namesake. Atlas Peak vineyards are located in the Napa Valley.

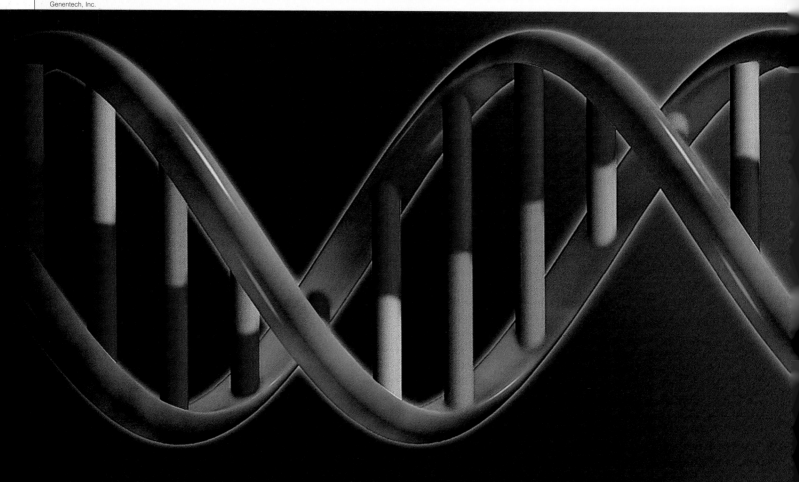

On the more artistic side, the Bay Area has been home to such internationally-renowned luminaries as Isadora Duncan, the pioneer of modern choreography, and Alice Walker, the Pulitzer Prize winning author.

Contemporary female tycoons include Suzy Tomkins, co-founder and owner of Esprit de Corps. Tomkins took the sportswear firm from its humble beginnings as the Plain Jane Dress Company to its present status as the nation's most successful such business by following a formula that demands the marketing of "lifestyle" to a young, energetic, upscale market. Esprit's product now represents the distinctive California look in 25 countries around the world.

Other forward-thinking Bay Area companies include Delta Dental, which built the nation's first, and most successful, dental-insurance plan; Koret of California — inventor of permanent-press clothing; and one of the best-known corporate citizens of Silicon Valley, the Intel Corporation, which combined two of its great inventions — programmable microprocessors and erasable, programmable memory — to create the personal computer as we know it today.

The United States' shift from a primarily industrial infrastructure to one built on the processing, retrieval, and sharing of information has been fueled by the kind of research, innovation, and creativity that has been the foundation of the idea-oriented Bay Area economy for some 200 years.

The San Francisco Bay Area is a leader in the biosciences industry. More than half of all California biotechnology firms, including Genentech, the world's largest biotechnology firm, are headquartered in the Bay Area. Genentech created the world's first recombinant DNA. Two of the three national centers mapping the human genetic system are located here.

COUNTERCULTURE CENTRAL

To many, "San Francisco" and "the sixties" are practically synonymous. In the 1950s, Haight and Ashbury were two obscure streets in a quiet, middle-class neighborhood near the "Panhandle" of Golden Gate Park. By the middle of the next decade, theirs were the signposts marking the birthplace of a revolution that rocked all the City — and all the world, as well.

Free spirits, mostly young, flocked into "The Haight" from across the country and every corner of the earth. Quickly dubbed "hippies" by the media, they came looking for enlightenment — through drugs, sex, eastern mysticism, acid rock and protest/folk music. Their philosophy generally espoused non-violence, personal freedom, fellowship, and disgust with modern society. They came to the famous Fillmore West for concerts, and they came to Golden Gate Park to listen to the Grateful Dead (surely The City's premier contribution to the rock world) play for free. They staged protests on the Vietnam war from the UC Berkeley campus to the downtown streets of San Francisco. They experimented with substances, lifestyles, and themselves. Many were runaways, not all of whom found the freedom and happiness they were looking for. A good percentage of these truth-seeking souls still live in the Bay Area, and others all over the world remember the days when people going to San Francisco were advised to wear some flowers in their hair.

WOMEN AND ART IN SAN FRANCISCO

Isadora Duncan

Isadora Duncan (1878-1927), was a pioneer in modern choreography. Born and reared in San Francisco by an agnostic mother who was permissive even by today's standards, Isadora shocked nineteenth-century audiences — defying all the conventions of classical ballet with which they were so familiar — by performing barefoot in a loose tunic. "The toast of two continents," she scandalized the public with her private life as well as her dance interpretations, bearing children to three different men, but not marrying until late in her life, when she wed a Russian Poet half her age. She died, at 39, still embracing the future, when the long scarf she was wearing became entangled in the wheel of the newfangled automobile in which she was riding, strangling her.

Alice Walker

In addition to winning a Pulitzer Prize for her acclaimed 1983 novel, The Color Purple, Alice Walker has enjoyed a literary career which has included academic appointments at Yale, Brandeis, Wellesley, Tougaloo College, and UC Berkeley; as well as an editorship at Ms. Magazine.

San Francisco's towers of finance prepare for dusk as sunset paints the sky. The buildings etched in lights are the towers of the Embarcadero Center.

San Francisco Convention & Visitors Bureau; Photographer-Kerrick James

*Perched on the church steps, children are
ready for Columbus Day pageantry.*

San Francisco Convention & Visitors Bureau

PEOPLE OF THE BAY AREA

The Bay Area makes up the nation's fourth-largest metropolitan market — and its six million residents are among the area's greatest assets.

As previously noted, these are people who tend to be younger, wealthier, and better-educated than the average American. In fact, 25 percent of local adults have completed four or more years of college, compared to just 16 percent nationally.

They are also more likely to hold administrative, technical, or professional positions. Median household income is nearly 28 percent higher than the national average — the highest in the country. They use that income to buy more telephone answering machines and compact-disc players per household than residents of any other metropolitan area in the U.S. At least 20 percent of the population uses personal computers, and such electronic conveniences as microwave ovens and TV remotes are found in 80 percent of local homes.

Women here are more likely to work than those in other large cities; a tradition dating back to the Gold Rush, when Jenny Wimmer performed the first amateur assay to confirm that it was indeed gold that had been discovered on the American River.

As America's most ethnically diverse region, the Bay Area can point with pride to large immigrant and first-generation communities of Asians, Europeans, and Latin Americans. The tolerance and adaptability such ethnic and cultural diversity demands are an important ingredient in the ambiance that makes the region so unique. Whereas the last census lists 22 percent of U.S. residents as belonging to ethnic minorities, the Bay Area is 35 percent, and in San Francisco itself, 53 percent.

San Francisco Convention & Visitors Bureau

These delightful women are taking part in the Columbus Day parade.

San Francisco Convention & Visitors Bureau

The Dragon takes to the streets in Chinatown.

A 1969 gift from the Republic of China, the dragon-crested gate at Grant Avenue and Bush Street is the front door to San Francisco's colorful, clangorous Chinatown.

The largest and fastest-growing ethnic group here is Asian — in fact, this is the only metropolitan area in the country in which Asians make up the biggest minority. These traditionally high achievers comprise 28 percent of the population. In 1990, they constituted only 15 percent, but still managed to account for an impressive 26 percent of the undergraduate student body at the University of California, Berkeley campus. With their strong work ethic, cultural disposition to education and research, and talent for entrepreneurship, Asians are naturals for the Bay Area economy.

But the region's high achievers are not restricted to any one group. The Bay Area can claim 30 Nobel Prize winners (one for every 200,000 residents): 12 in physics, 10 in chemistry, 3 each in physiology/medicine and economics, and 2 in literature. Also living here are 2 winners of the Enrico Fermi Award, 34 MacArthur Fellowship recipients, 18 Pulitzer Prize winners, 237 Fellows of the National Academy of Science, 229 Academy of Arts & Sciences Fellows, and 549 recipients of Guggenheim Fellowships.

Statistics alone really cannot provide a clear picture of the people of the Bay Area, and what makes them unique. But perhaps one telling anecdote can. On May 4, 1987, the beloved Golden Gate Bridge marked its 50th birthday. Traffic was halted at dawn to clear the span for a massive San Francisco-style extravaganza in which 300,000 pedestrians loaded the bridge to three times the weight of normal rush-hour traffic — some 45 million pounds — and another half-million spectators crowded the bridge approaches and nearby viewpoints. At dusk, these and tens of thousands more were treated to a pyrotechnic display in which fireworks cascaded 400 feet from the bridge towers to the Bay below. This gargantuan birthday party caused the bridge's suspension cables to stretch a full ten feet, and the gracefully-arched roadway to flatten beneath the weight. A tribute to the inspired engineering design of Joseph Strauss is the fact that neither the great bridge nor any of the approximately one million revelers who came to pay homage that day sustained any serious damage.

Yes, San Francisco knows how to throw a party. San Franciscans also know how to extract the maximum value from ideas — and that is why the Bay Area is leading the world into the 21st century.

Kent Bostick, member of Team Shaklee, was at age 43 the oldest member of the 1996 United States Olympic Cycling Team.

Shaklee Corporation

FEEDING BODY AND SOUL

A revolution in American cooking started with the 1971 opening, in Berkeley, of Chez Panisse, founded by Alice Waters. Combining the finest French recipes with the freshest American ingredients, Chez Panisse is consistently ranked among the country's top ten restaurants. One of Waters' former chefs, Jeremiah Towers, went on to become the owner of the equally successful Stars restaurant in San Francisco.

The Bay Area also enjoys the inspirational presence of spiritual leaders like the Reverend Cecil Williams, pastor of Glide Memorial Methodist Church for a quarter-century. His work in ministering to America's most economically and ethnically diverse congregation has given birth to dozens of nationally-emulated programs for the disadvantaged.

DES Architects + Engineers; Photographer-Christopher Irion

Stars' Palo Alto Restaurant-Piano Bar; Palo Alto, California.

CHINATOWN MORE THAN A MOVIE

The largest settlement of its kind outside mainland China, Chinatown is a place of special magic for all who love the City, and it has its roots in the same events that launched the rest of San Francisco: the great Gold Rush of 1848, and the laborious building of the first transcontinental railroad.

The first significant immigrant population to leave China for San Francisco were drawn by the Gold Rush. They came to handle the menial work for the prospectors and merchants — including laundry, which was quite a luxury for San Franciscans, some of whom had actually been sending their shirts to Honolulu via clipper ship for laundering and pressing. In 1852, there were about 25,000 Chinese in the state, but that number had swelled to 105,465 by 1880. At first, they were regarded as a welcome addition to a very small work force that was struggling to work the gold fields and build railroads while still lumbering, farming, and carrying on commerce. As local prosperity increased, the Chinese began to be viewed as a serious competitive threat. When the Depression of 1873 started, things got worse. Over the next few decades, the Chinese in California were subjected to citizen riots, discriminatory laws, and general ill-will. In fact, the Chinese Exclusion Act of 1882 was not repealed until 1943, when the World War Two alliance between the U.S. and China made it an embarrassment.

Today, the great contributions made to U.S. society in general, and San Francisco in particular, by the immigrant Chinese are finally being recognized — and what was once looked upon as a somewhat sinister and dangerously "foreign" district of opium dens and Tong wars has at last come to be seen as a delightfully exotic place to shop, eat, or just stroll along soaking up the Asian atmosphere — a favorite sightseeing destination for visitors, and just another neighborhood (albeit an unusual one) to the people who live here.

This Bay Area kitten gets into the spirit of Halloween.

Wyndham Images

Embarcadero Center.

Photographer-Paul Langland

LEADERS IN BUSINESS AND INDUSTRY

The story of San Francisco is the story of entrepreneurs, from the farmers who created the state's $40 billion agribusiness empire to the high-tech whiz kids who built Silicon Valley. The world's best and brightest are attracted to the area by the business opportunities, economic health, and quality of life available here.

In this information-driven age, Bay Area businesses have discovered the competitive advantages bestowed by commitment to human resources, and the value to be derived from research and other creative processes. The broad range of companies that have found or made profitable niches in the region's economic picture is a testament to the economic diversity and growth-oriented attitudes of the entire Bay Area.

CORPORATE HEADQUARTERS

The convenient location and commerce-friendly atmosphere of the San Francisco Bay Area have helped to establish the highest concentration of Fortune 500-company headquarters outside New York City — including such industry giants as Apple, Hewlett-Packard, Intel, and National Semiconductor. Also among the world's biggest and most successful companies headquartered here are Bankamerica, Bechtel, Chevron, Clorox, Del Monte, Levi Strauss, and Wells Fargo.

GOVERNMENT ADMINISTRATION

Historically, San Francisco has always served as the center of commerce and industry in the western U.S. This has led to the Bay Area's selection as the site for many governmental entities, both State and Federal. The State government's presence includes the California Public Utilities Commission, and the State Departments of Insurance, Banking, and Saving & Loans; while the State's judiciary arm is represented by the California Supreme Court and other appellate courts.

Two of the three California offices of the Federal Communications Commission (FCC) are located in San Francisco, as are the Securities and Exchange Commission (SEC), Federal Reserve Bank, and Federal Home Loan Bank. The U.S. District Court, and the Ninth Circuit Court of Appeals, are to be found here as well.

The Wine Alliance; Photographer-M.J. Wickham

The wine caves of Atlas Peak Vineyards are tunneled into the volcanic cliffs surrounding the property.

Walgreens Woodland Distribution Center-Automated Distribution; Woodland, California.

DES Architects + Engineers; Photographer-Jane Lidz

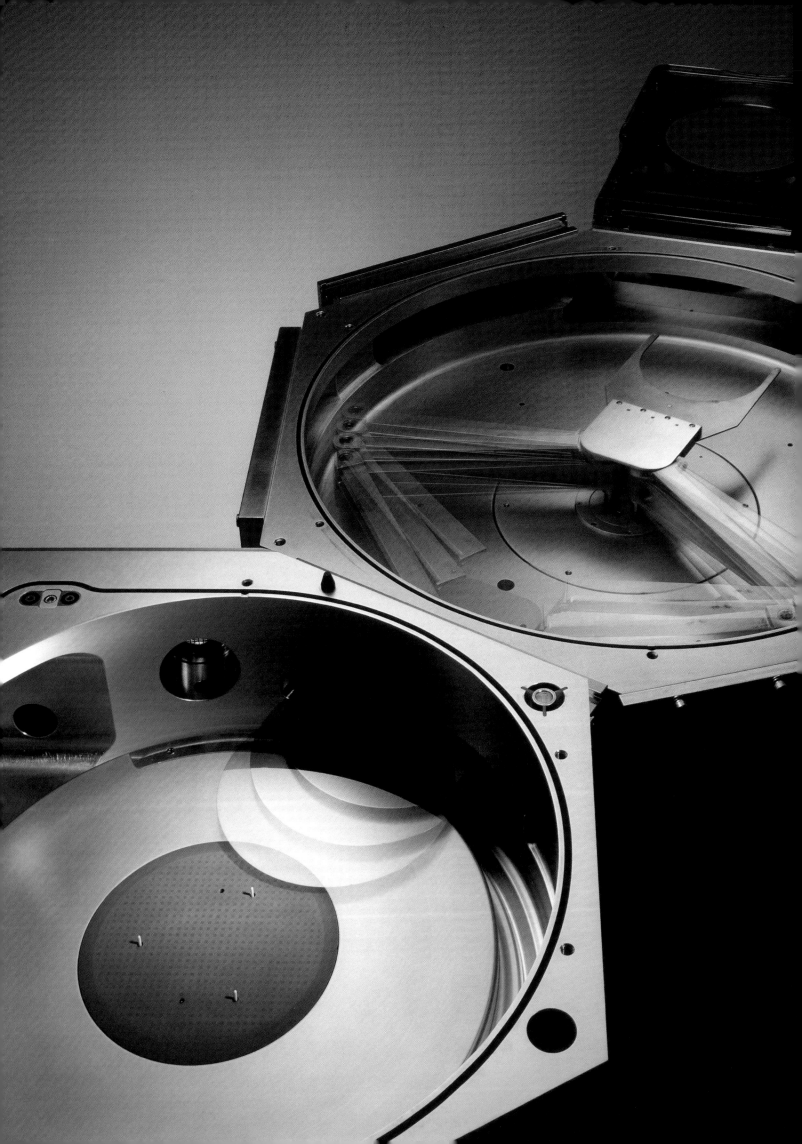

Lam Research Corporation's Deep SubMicron™ (DSM™) 9900 HPD CVD system deposits superior quality insulating films between metal layers for intermetal dielectric applications.

PROFESSIONAL SERVICES

The exceptionally strong professional-services industry of the Bay Area help make San Francisco a center for international deal-making. Seven of the ten largest law firms in California are headquartered here, and each of the nation's Big Six accounting firms maintain multiple Bay Area offices. There are several hundred consulting organizations operating in the area, with the country's premier management-consulting companies among them. This kind of business can only benefit from the area's highly-educated labor force, central location, and concentration of governmental bodies.

Besides providing a large local market for professional-services firms, the Bay Area offers easy access to overseas markets, thanks to its three international airports and the availability of state-of-the-art telecommunications facilities. These amenities also make it easier for clients from places as geographically diverse as Europe and the Pacific Rim countries to conduct their business — electronically or in person — at this ever-alluring destination.

MANUFACTURING

The manufacturing base of the Bay Area consists primarily of products and techniques high on the value-added list: computer components and peripherals; semiconductor manufacturing systems and the goods they produce; satellite and microwave communications technology; and instruments for scientific measurement and analysis. While many of these firms, such as Apple and Hewlett-Packard, are household words all over the world, some of the biggest — Intel, Hexcel, LSI Logic, OCU, and Varian — specialize mostly in business-to-business marketing.

But high-tech isn't the whole story. 25 percent to 35 percent of California's chemicals, machinery, fabricated metals, and refined petroleum are produced in the Bay Area, as are 20 percent to 25 percent of the state's apparel and food products. The printing and publishing industries also thrive here; and a variety of small-scale manufacturers have found their places in the local economy by taking advantage of specialized labor pools and specific demand, and by working together with other Bay Area industries.

MEDICINE AND THE BIOSCIENCES

As previously noted, the Bay Area was the birthplace, in 1974, of the biotechnology industry, with the discovery of recombinant DNA. Close cooperation between world-renowned research institutions and private commercial companies has created the area's leadership position in the research, development, and marketing of products and applications in the agriculture, medical, and production fields. The professional climate has enabled the industry to attract the human and material resources necessary for sustained growth. For example, the University of California, San Francisco, conducts more research for the National Institutes of Health than any other institution, public or private; and two of the three national centers attempting to map the human genome are located here.

More than half of all California biotechnology firms — including Genentech, the world's largest — are headquartered in the Bay Area.

After going through the entire process in New United Motor's Body & Weld Department, over 3,800 welds will have been applied to each auto body.

REAL ESTATE

The Bay Area hosts some of the country's leading sales, development, and property-management firms. Nearly 20 percent of the office space in downtown San Francisco is owned or managed by the Shorenstein Company. Catellus, which inherited much of the land acquired by the Southern Pacific Railroad in the 19th century, is one of the largest real-estate developers in the U.S. Major home builders in the area include Hayman Homes, the Hoffman Company, and Sunset Development.

INSURANCE

In addition to the companies covered in Chapter Two, like Delta Dental and Kaiser Permanente, the locally-headquartered insurance industry includes firms such as Transamerica (the nation's largest provider of specialized insurance services), the California State Automobile Association, Fireman's Fund, Industrial Indemnity, Argonaut, California Blue Shield, and the California Casualty Group.

ARCHITECTURE, ENGINEERING, AND CONSTRUCTION

The Bay Area has a solid tradition of leadership in architecture, engineering, and construction. It is presently home to Bechtel Group, the nation's largest engineering construction firm, and Gensler and Associates, the largest architectural company in the U.S. San Francisco designers and builders have worked on some of the world's most ambitious and challenging projects. Among these ranks the regional infrastructure which includes the Bay Bridge, Bay Area Rapid Transit system (BART), and the massive Hetch Hetchy water and power project. Such innovations in their times as steel-reinforced concrete, the perfection of steel-plate welding, and the entire environmental-design movement have their roots in local history.

The architects and engineers of the Bay Area are supported by outstanding educational resources and a highly-specialized labor pool. Two of every three California engineers, one of every six U.S. architects, and one in every seven Fellows of the National Academy of Engineering can be found here.

MEDIA AND PUBLISHING

As America's fourth-largest media market, the Bay Area is internationally significant, with its 85 radio stations, 22 broadcast television stations, and 1.1 million cable TV subscribers. Local media publish 348 periodicals targeting the regional market, with a combined circulation of more than 12.5 million. Another 127 periodicals, aimed at national and international markets, account for an additional 15.5 million in combined circulation.

From its earliest days, the Bay Area has been home to a society of readers. This is why the region boasts more independent presses than any other U.S. Metropolitan area except New York. Innovative local publishers include companies such as Nolo Press, whose do-it-yourself law series launched a "paralegal revolution" in will-preparation, divorce-filing, and other common legal activities.

DESIGN

The design industry in the Bay Area encompasses a wide variety of disciplines: architecture (see above), interiors, public spaces, historic preservation, landscaping, urban planning, advertising, apparel, graphics and photography, computer software and hardware, scientific instruments, commercial products and packaging, and many more.

For three decades, our images of corporate America have been created in San Francisco by Walter Landor and Landor Associates. Almost every commercial aircraft in the sky proudly bears a Landor design on its tail.

Computer technology from the Bay Area helps keep the U.S. on the cutting edge of worldwide electronics and data-processing competition, and local firms like IDEO and Frog/Esslinger are international leaders in product design, especially of medical instruments. The foundation of contemporary Bay Area design is a history that includes such well-known products and processes as Postscript printer language, generations of Levis jeans, and even the humble bobby-pin.

POWER, NATURAL RESOURCES, AND ENVIRONMENTAL SERVICES

The special role in the Bay Area economy played by natural resources began, of course, with the Gold Rush. Gold banked by the 49ers provided seed money for some of America's most successful enterprises. To start with, the California Electric Light Company built the world's

San Francisco's temples of finance seen from a balustraded parapet on Russian hill above the Broadway tunnel. The silvery Bay Bridge stretches toward Oakland in the background.

Jill Davis, winemaker, and Ed Blacamonte of William Hill Winery remove red grape skins from fermenter before sending them to the press.

first electric-power-generating plant in San Francisco in 1879 — an effort that would later give rise to the nation's biggest power utility, Pacific Gas & Electric (PG&E). Then, in 1900, Standard Oil of California built what was then the world's largest oil refinery on the shores of the Bay, paving the way for one of the country's most prominent petroleum refiners and marketers, Chevron. A concerned and committed corporate citizen, Chevron employs more than 400 specialists to monitor the environmental and health aspects of its own operations, while annually contributing more than $200 million to programs for ecological monitoring, research, and public education.

But then, San Franciscans have always been as concerned with protecting and conserving natural resources as with developing them. The great explorer and naturalist, John Muir, founded the Sierra Club here in 1892, launching a movement that has profoundly affected the way in which the modern world views the natural environment. With a history like this, it is easy to see why Bay Area power and natural-resource firms are considered the world's leading innovators in environmental conservation. The area's plants, which produce power from wind and geothermal sources, are the world's most productive. The Bay Area is home to the Electric Power Research Institute — a cooperative venture of more than 600 utilities, dedicated to more efficient power production and the development of renewable energy resources.

But environmental concern is more than a movement — it is a business opportunity. The country's largest concentration of environmental consulting, product, and service companies is located here, and the environmental-law practice of most major U.S. law firms is based in San Francisco. That adds up to 90 private law firms, 13 public-interest law firms, and 22 government entities concerned with the environment; plus 165 consulting firms specializing in natural-resource management, environmental and geotechnical engineering, and forestry and water-systems management. To put it simply, Bay Area companies are in the vanguard of corporations around the world that are working to control potential pollution at the source — for the sake of good business, as well as of life on earth itself.

AGRIBUSINESS AND FOOD

Some of the United States' largest growing, processing, packaging, marketing, and distribution businesses are located in the Bay Area, including both of California's Fortune 500 agribusiness firms, Tri Valley Growers and Sun Diamond Growers. Other major players based in the area are: Basic American Foods, Continental Companies, C&H Sugar, Del Monte, Dole, Folgers, Golden Grain, Granny Goose, Hills Brothers, Kikkoman USA, MJB Coffee, and Spreckels, to name just a few.

California, as a whole, enjoys a $20 billion agricultural-production industry (the nation's most diverse, and one which is over 60 percent larger than that of any other state). The Bay Area is located in the heart of the most productive and varied agricultural region on earth — and a significant percentage of America's field crops, fruits, nuts, flowers, and premium wines are produced by the farms, orchards, and vineyards within a 200-mile radius of San Francisco. Support for the industry comes both from the world's leading agricultural research institution, the University of California, Davis (where, for example, more than 50 new strains of strawberry were developed), and from the close proximity of California's two biggest agricultural lenders, Bankamerica and Wells Fargo. Individual agribusiness firms and product-marketing boards receive the benefits of San Francisco's well-developed trade infrastructure, as well as deal-making support from the professional services community.

The more than 250 cash crops produced in California include many that are not grown commercially anywhere else in North America, including almonds, artichokes, dates, figs, kiwi fruit, olives, pistachios, pomegranates, prunes, and raisins.

VITICULTURE

A mild, Mediterranean-type climate and rolling, hilly terrain allow the Bay Area to produce the nation's best wines, and the region's many micro-climates provide for an extraordinary variety in viticulture. Pinot noir and chardonnay grapes flourish in mountain gaps cooled by coastal fogs and ocean breezes, while cabernet sauvingnon and chenin blanc vines bear their finest fruit on the warmer acreage a few miles inland. These excellent conditions allow the Bay Area to produce 40 percent of California's $700 million wine-grape crop, on just 21 percent of the state's wine-growing acreage.

FLORICULTURE

San Mateo County's warm days, cool but frost-free nights, and nearness to San Francisco International Airport make it the center of the Bay Area's $300 million floricultural industry — but flowers also make up at least a million-dollar crop in each of the area's counties, including densely-developed San Francisco.

VISITOR INDUSTRY

San Francisco has long been the favorite city of American travelers — and one of the most popular in the world, second only to Paris. More than 14 million people visit The City each year, collectively spending $5 billion. These revenues provide direct employment for more than 60,000 area residents, and help to make the visitor industry San Francisco's largest.

Bank of Canton of California

Bank of Canton of California's San Francisco Chinatown branch dates back to 1909. Its classic design makes it one of the most visited buildings in San Francisco.

Port of San Francisco

The Crystal Symphony *passes Alcatraz
as the ship cruises the bay.*

A little more than half of this economic impact is generated by visitors staying overnight in local hotels, 30 percent of whom list foreign addresses. The tourist trade throughout northern California is anchored by San Francisco's main visitor groups — those attending meetings and conventions, transient commercial guests, and vacation travelers. The economic contributions of these visitors also help to support the staggering number of shops, restaurants, and great entertainment opportunities available to Bay Area residents and guests alike.

INTERNATIONAL TRADE

The magnificent harbors of San Francisco Bay have attracted international trade, a mainstay of the local economy, since the 18th century. Today, a full range of maritime activity takes place in four major ports on the Bay, and five more along the Sacramento River. The growing importance of high-value trade goods, however, has helped to shift the balance of international shipping from sea to air. The current annual value of air cargo cleared through the San Francisco Customs District is nearly 20 percent greater than that of seaborne cargo — and the gap is widening each year. The many trading companies and professional-services firms based in the City handle the business end of trade (as opposed to actual physical movement of goods) smoothly and efficiently.

Silicon Valley electronics firms, as well as some of the area's apparel giants like Levi Strauss, Esprit de Corps, and The Gap, have forged strong ties with the growing economies of Pacific Rim countries through contracts for offshore manufacturing. These ties are often reinforced by family connections within the Bay Area's large Asian population.

CULTURE AND THE ARTS

Since the Gold Rush, the arts and entertainment have been an integral part of San Francisco life. Even during the disastrous days from 1848 to 1851, when virtually the entire city burned to the ground six times, theaters and concert halls were always among the first structures to be rebuilt. Then, as now, the City was a magnet for creative talent in the literary, visual, and performing arts. The abundant opportunities available here to both artists and audiences have sparked the formation of more than 1,000 different arts-oriented organizations, representing many different cultures and every level of professionalism. A more detailed view of the City's unique artistic and cultural ambiance may be found in Chapter Seven.

While San Francisco is generally considered the cultural hub of the region, the Bay Area's other cities boast a variety of museums, theaters, and musical ensembles of their own. Stanford University, for example, exhibits the country's premier collection of Rodin sculpture; the Berkeley Repertory Theatre has a long-standing reputation; and many area communities have either constructed, or plan to construct, performing arts centers to accommodate the arts groups active in the region.

LIGHTS! CAMERA! ACTION!

Well before Hollywood began its reign as the world's movie capital, the picturesque little South Bay town of Niles was the favorite film location. Niles was the site of most of Charlie Chaplin's early pictures, including the silent classic, *The Tramp*. In the five years between 1911 and 1916, Essanay Studios produced more than 450 silent one-reelers in Niles. These featured most of the great stars of the era — Chaplin, Bronco Billy Anderson, Wallace Beery, Marie Dressler, Zazu Pitts, and Ben Turpin.

Of course, San Francisco itself has lent its aura and remarkable settings to scores of movies, TV productions, and commercials. Think of the often-imitated but never-duplicated car chase in *Bullit*, Clint Eastwood's rooftop fight in *Dirty Harry*, the wild beauty of the bay and city skyline in *On The Beach*, the grimness of San Quentin in *48 Hours*, and the small-town ambiance Santa Rosa lent to *American Graffitti*. Then, of course, there is George Lucas, writer and director of *Star Wars*, the film that, in 1977, expanded the frontiers of sound design and revolutionary special effects, shattered all previous box-office records, won seven Academy Awards, and established Lucas as the industry's most prominent pioneer in the fields of visual and sound technology.

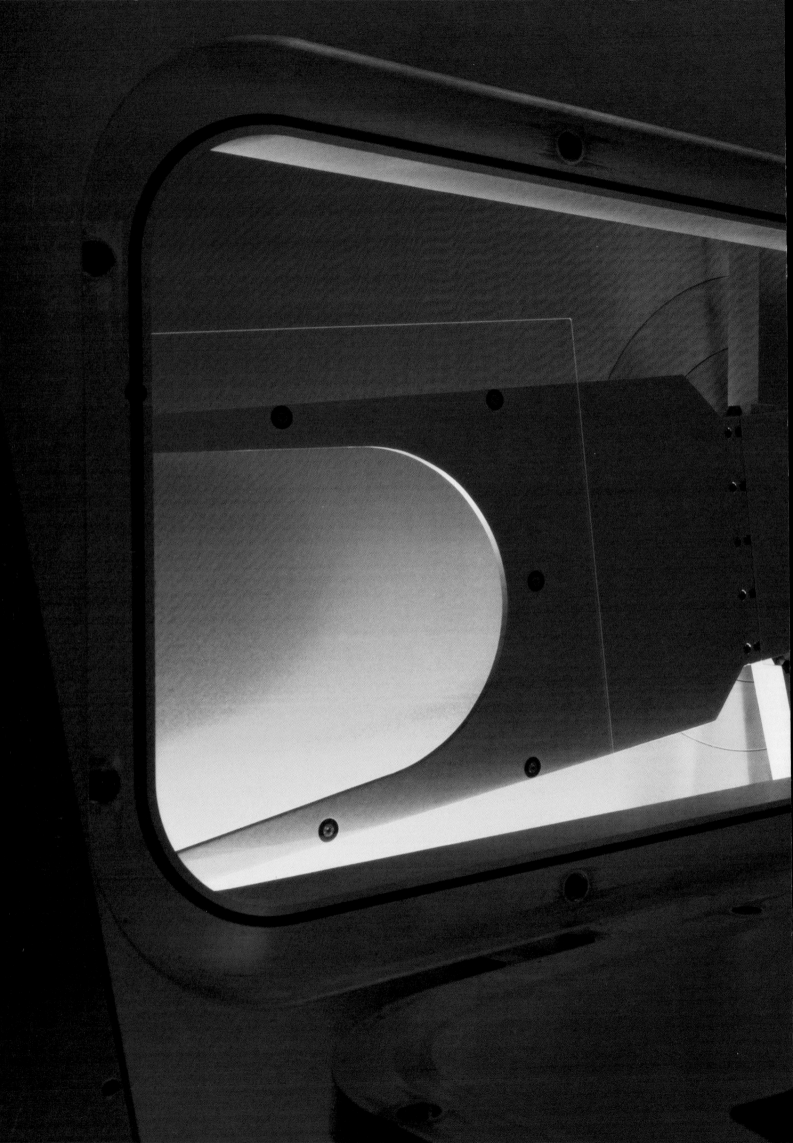

*Continuum™, Lam Research
Corporation's new flat panel display etch
system, leverages the production-proven
Transformer Coupled Plasma™ (TCP™)
scalable technology for third-generation
processing of large glass substrates up to
600 mm x 720 mm.*

EDUCATION AND RESEARCH

As noted in Chapter One, the information-based economy of the Bay Area rests on a solid foundation of education and research. Higher education, both public and private, helps to produce the nation's most educated labor force; and the region's exceptionally productive research community includes academic institutions and government-sponsored National laboratories, as well as non-profit organizations and the research campuses of some of America's most successful companies.

PUBLIC HIGHER EDUCATION

Each year, the State of California provides college education to nearly two million full- and part-time students, on 135 campuses. This constitutes the largest higher-education system in the world. Included in this system are two-year community colleges, emphasizing academic and skills training; California State Universities, offering undergraduate studies; and the University of California, which specializes in research and graduate education.

The cream of the state's public higher education system is undoubtedly the University of California, and three of its nine campuses are located in the Bay Area. UC Berkeley, with its 30,000 students, is the nation's premier public university, having 30 graduate and 62 undergraduate departments ranked in the national "top 10."

UC San Francisco, serving about 4,000 students, is the top-ranked public medical school in the country, doing more research for the National Institutes of Health than any other institution, public or private. UC Davis, a noted research institution, leads the nation in undergraduate and graduate schools of agricultural sciences and agribusiness, and has 20,000 students.

Four of the 19 campuses of the California State University system are also located in the Bay Area: CSU at Hayward, San Francisco State, San Jose State, and Sonoma State. All offer both undergraduate and graduate degrees.

The Bay Area is home to 27 of California's 107 community college campuses, offering educational opportunities to an amazing 350,000 students, both full and part-time.

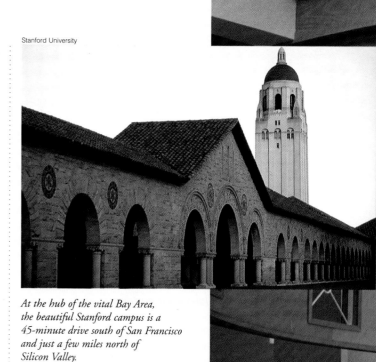

Stanford University

At the hub of the vital Bay Area, the beautiful Stanford campus is a 45-minute drive south of San Francisco and just a few miles north of Silicon Valley.

Sequoia Hospital Acute Care Facility-Rehab and Physical Therapy; Redwood City, California.

DES Architects + Engineers; Photographer-Vittoria Visuals

Lam Research Corporation's Transformer Coupled Plasma™ (TCP™) 9100 high-density oxide system provides process repeatability over a wide range of oxide processes at twice the etch rates of competitive offerings.

PRIVATE HIGHER EDUCATION

Dozens of private colleges and universities can be found in the Bay Area, including such world-renowned schools as Stanford University and Mills College for women in Oakland. There are 19 local schools with religious affiliations also available.

Stanford University

Stanford University claims an enrollment of approximately 12,000. The University has the distinction of providing 24 graduate and 37 undergraduate departments in nation's "top 10."

Graduate Theological Union

This consortium of nine member schools and 12 affiliates represents three world religions (Berkeley).

Medicine

UC San Francisco — schools of Medicine, Dentistry, Pharmacy, Nursing

Stanford University School of Medicine

UC Davis — schools of Medicine, Veterinary Medicine

University of the Pacific School of Dentistry (San Francisco)

California College of Podiatric Medicine (San Francisco)

Law

Boalt Hall School of Law (Berkeley)

Stanford School of Law

Hastings College of the Law (UC System, San Francisco)

UC Davis School of Law

University of San Francisco Law School

Santa Clara University Law School

Golden Gate University Law School (San Francisco)

Marine Technology

California Maritime Academy (Vallejo)

PRIMARY AND SECONDARY EDUCATION

The Bay Area is home to one-third of California's top 100 public high schools, and nearly 1,500 accredited private schools. With only one-fifth of the total state population, the area produces one-third of California's National Merit Scholars, and more than two-thirds of local high-school graduates go on to college.

RESEARCH

The most productive research community in the U.S. is located in the Bay Area. Sixteen of the elements in the Periodic Table were discovered at UC Berkeley alone. The foundations of Silicon Valley — home to one-third of Fortune 500 computer firms — were laid by electronics research performed at Stanford. The birth of biotechnology can be traced to a conversation in a deli between UC's Herbert Boyer and Stanford's Stanley Cohen. The far-reaching influence of UC Davis agricultural research is felt around the world, and is responsible for creation of the "Green Revolution," as well as having had tremendous impact on California's $50 billion agribusiness and food industry.

University of California, Berkeley

- 80 independent research units conducting $223 million worth of research annually
- Plutonium and all 16 transuranic elements discovered here, as well as the anti-proton, which confirmed existence of anti-matter
- First to create photosynthesis outside a living cell
- First to isolate and crystallize a virus
- Developer of the Ames test, worldwide standard for identifying carcinogens

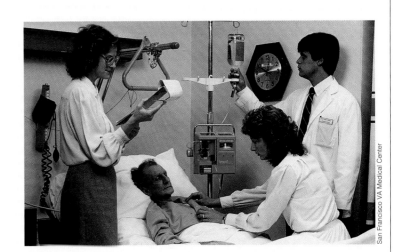

Veterans receive high quality care from multi-disciplinary medical teams at the San Francisco VA Medical Center.

Lawrence Berkeley Laboratory

- National Research Laboratory, operated by the University of California under contract to the U.S. Department of Energy

- Employs 4,300 people to conduct $210 million worth of research annually

- Research plant includes three major accelerators, electron micro-scopes, controlled environments, alloy development and test facility, and a 55,000-volume library

- Has conducted acclaimed research in high-energy physics, fusion, superconductivity, computer science, molecular biology, X-ray optics, and radiation

Lawrence Livermore Laboratory

- National Research Laboratory, operated by the University of California under contract to the U.S. Department of Energy

- Annual budget of $1.2 billion

- Employs 10,000 people, approximately half each on energy research and nuclear weapons research

Lam Research Corporation's Advanced Capability Alliance™ multichamber platform offers an open, modular design which allows easy access to all components for maintenance and serviceability.

- Major projects: laser and magnetic fusion, coal gasification, oil shale retorting, biomedical and environmental research, electric-automobile power cells, geothermal energy, nuclear waste disposal, and atmospheric pollution modeling

University of California, Davis

- 45 independent research units, conducting $135 million worth of research annually

- Major impact on agriculture worldwide - developed 24 new table grape varieties, 30 new kinds of strawberry, the mechanical tomato harvester, and many disease-resistant plant strains

University of California, San Francisco

- Eleven independent research units, with 1,500 laboratories conducting more than 2,000 projects annually, at a cost of $185 million

- Consistently conducts more research funded by the National Institute of Health than any other institution

- Developed recombinant DNA technology to launch biotech industry

- Developed synthetic human growth hormone

- Pioneered fetal surgery

Stanford University

- Eighty independent research units, conducting $433 million worth of research annually

- Driver of Silicon Valley electronics development

- Isolated human immunity gene

- Developed synthetic viral DNA

- Major research in subatomic particle physics, polymers, linear programming, and artificial intelligence

NASA Ames Research Center

- Life sciences research center for NASA, located in Mountain View

- Annual budget of $645 million

- Aeronautics — computer simulation, fluid mechanics

- Astronautics — spacecraft development, space sciences and Earth applications.

- Research into human efficiency in space, space medicine, advanced life-support systems, and extraterrestrial-life detection

Sandia National Laboratories

■ Operated by AT&T for U.S. Department of Energy, located in Livermore

■ Annual budget of $140 million

■ Employs 1,000 people, half each on nuclear weapons research and solar energy, combustion, and public-private technology transfer

SRI International

■ Non-profit, independent research & development organization, headquartered in Palo Alto

■ Annually employs 1,500 people in more than 100 disciplines, to conduct $270 million worth of research projects

■ Conducts research on artificial intelligence, physical & life sciences, and public policy.

Interdisciplinary Collaboration

Experimentation in many different fields allows Bay Area scientists and researchers to cooperate, to cross-fertilize ideas and discoveries in many different disciplines. For instance Frostban, a bacteria which inhibits frost formation on strawberries, involves the sciences of meteorology, biology, and botany; Magnetic Resonance Imaging (MRI) marries nuclear physics, medicine, and electronics, to create one of today's most important medical-diagnostic tools; and computer-aided design (CAD) systems unite electronics with basic design principles to automate routine drafting tasks.

Innovators in Research

Many firms not headquartered in the Bay Area have established research facilities here, because of the commitment to research and development demonstrated by Bay Area companies. Among them are:

CIBA-Geigy — Laser Products Division

Dow Chemical — Western Applied Science & Technology Labs

IBM Almaden Research Center

IBM San Jose Research Center

Litton Industries — Applied Technology Division

Lockheed Palo Alto Research Laboratories

National Food Processors — Western Research Laboratory

North America Philips Research Laboratory

Sandoz Crop Protection Research Division

United Technologies — Chemical Systems Division

Xerox Palo Alto Research Center

Researchers at the University of California San Francisco are in the forefront of genetic research on severe hemophilia.

US News and World Report's *latest survey of America's best medical schools ranked UCSF sixth overall among research-oriented schools, and number one in the Western United States. Shown is a biochemistry class for first year medical students.*

*The Bay Bridge, seen here against the
backdrop of San Francisco's magnificent
downtown skyline, links Oakland to
San Francisco.*

San Francisco Convention & Visitors Bureau;
Photographer-Kerrick James

Chapter Six

EVERYONE'S FAVORITE CITY

EVERYONE'S FAVORITE CITY

The San Francisco Bay Area is home to over 6.5 million people, and is visited by more than 4 million each year. We can try to answer the question: Why? What is it about this "Baghdad by the Bay" that is so perennially attractive to so many?

Well, to begin with, it is beautiful. San Francisco's Mediterranean-type setting is enhanced by its remarkable range of architecture, from lovingly-restored Victorian homes to futuristic skyscrapers. Tree-lined streets, steep hills, dozens of parks, colorful street life, bustling wharves, and water, water everywhere, all combine to give the City a distinctively European flavor — especially at night, when a million lights set the city ablaze.

More than 700,000 acres of open space in the Bay Area is owned by the public (about 16 percent of all land in the metropolitan area). Parks and recreational areas account for nearly 60 percent of these lands, with 20 percent for watersheds, and almost 15 percent devoted to plant and animal habitat. Development takes place in well-defined corridors separated by greenbelts, bringing the natural world close to every citizen, at work or at home.

Opportunities for sightseeing are abundant. From Golden Gate Park to Fisherman's Wharf; from Chinatown to the Mission district; there are always places to go, things to do, and fascinating people to meet — and, of course, there is always shopping.

Leading names in national retail are well-represented here. San Francisco's retail center includes major department stores; boutiques and specialty stores; ethnic shopping districts; multi-store complexes; well-known shopping areas such as Union Street and Union Square, which is ranked with 5th Avenue in New York City and Rodeo Drive

San Francisco Convention & Visitors Bureau; Photographer-Sandor Balantoni

Row upon row of working boats and sports fishing pleasure craft tie up at Fisherman's Wharf in San Francisco, famed for its bayview restaurants and seafood stands.

Fine San Francisco cuisine is equaled only by the excellent regional wines that accompany it.

The Wine Alliance: Callaway Vineyard & Winerya

This stretch of Russian Hill's Lombard Street didn't have a curve to call its own until 1922. That year, at a cost of $8,000, the city serpentined the steep stretch, creating "The World's Crookedest" street.

in Beverly Hills. The convenience of having such great variety concentrated in such a relatively small and easily accessible area has put San Francisco high on the list of desirable shopping destinations.

Wholesale trade also is a major industry with trade marts like Showplace Square (furniture and interiors), Contract Design Center (office/commercial furnishings), Gift Center (jewelry and value items), Diamond & Jewelry Mart, San Francisco Mart (kitchen, bath, carpet and furnishings), TechMart (computers, software and peripherals), Flower Mart, Apparel Mart, and Fashion Center. These large, permanent facilities are supplemented by trade shows and markets held in hotels and convention halls throughout the year.

For the 14 million who annually seek out The City for meetings and conventions, San Francisco offers 34 convention hotels with 240,000 square-feet of exhibition space, 600 meeting rooms, and 17,500 guest rooms; while tourist hotels add another 12,500 guest rooms. The Moscone Center, one of the country's premier convention venues, has 442,000 square feet of exhibition space, 138,000 square feet of meeting space, and banquet seating for 4,600 in its Esplanade Ballroom. There are also 80 other conference centers, exhibition halls, pavilions, and auditoriums within the City.

Theater, opera, ballet, music — whatever your idea of a good time, you can find it all, and love it all, in San Francisco.

A City Built On Gold

On February 2, 1848, the Treaty of Guadalupe Hidalgo officially transferred control of Alta (upper) California from Mexico to America. Just a few days earlier, gold had been discovered on the American River, at the site of a sawmill being built for the great landowner, Johann Sutter. Word spread quickly through California, and within a few months, the news was carried by ship and horse-messengers to the rest of the U.S. When the word finally hit the outside world in late 1848, the Gold Rush was officially on, and the adventurous men and women who would become famed as the 49ers were on their way west.

The settlement recently re-christened San Francisco was not much more than a sleepy little village with a minor military garrison in early 1848, before the Gold Rush exploded into its quiet existence. But by 1851, it had grown into one of the busiest and most populous cities in the world. Gold-seekers flooded in by the tens of thousands, along with those who wanted to supply, serve, entertain — and prey upon — the hopeful prospectors. Ships, abandoned by crews stricken with gold fever, filled the harbor, and prudent captains avoided entering the Bay at all. Some of these ships were used as floating hotels and even prisons — because of all the things San Francisco was lacking, living accommodations were in particularly short supply, as were law and order.

The Gold Rush certainly started off San Francisco's life as a U.S. possession with a bang. Fortunes were made and lost here, and residents came and went, but there was always a solid core of visionary citizens willing to expend their time, money, and effort to create the city of their dreams.

San Francisco Convention & Visitors Bureau; Photographer-Sophie Fleming

No, this isn't a windowsill out of Italy, but one in San Francisco's North Beach district. Rich in Italian heritage, the neighborhood (which is less than a square mile) today offers jazz clubs, galleries, family-style restaurants and delicatessens.

Bright-colored balloons festively decorate Ghirardelli Square, a multi-level miscellany of eating-shopping-entertainment enticements ensconced in a 19th century chocolate factory.

San Francisco Convention & Visitors Bureau; Courtesy Ghirardelli Square

SURVIVOR CITY

If there is one thing San Francisco has proved over the past 150 years, it's that you can't keep a good city down. At least, not for long.

The huge population explosion caused by the Gold Rush meant that hotels, restaurants, stores, and casinos were put up hastily, often using shoddy materials (when they were put up at all — a good many establishments were housed in tents). It is hardly surprising, then, that the town was swept by no fewer than six great fires between 1848 and 1851. Each time, the hardy survivors threw off the frightful financial and human losses, and began to build around what little was left. After every fire, The City rose anew; and fire-proofing and prevention grew better with each disaster.

But nothing could have prepared San Francisco, or the rest of the world, for what happened on April 18, 1906, when a mighty earthquake, now estimated at 8.3 on the Richter scale, tore the city apart. Nearly 500 people perished as great fires (caused by overturned woodstoves and broken gas pipes) raged out of control for three days, leaving the business and industrial districts leveled and charred, and thousands of residents either temporarily or permanently homeless.

Once again, San Francisco bounced back. And once again, there was a positive side to the disaster. Municipal building codes were strengthened, and the Fire Department was reorganized.

The recovery of The City from the Quake of '06 had some unexpected, and certainly unintended, consequences for later generations of San Franciscans. In order to show its triumph to the World by hosting the 1915 Panama Pacific International Exposition, the city used landfill from the quake to extend the Marina District into the Bay. For obvious reasons, the stability of this new-made land was questionable.

When the massive 7.1 Loma Prieta Earthquake (best known now as the World Series Quake) struck the Bay Area on October 17, 1989, the older two-to-four story housing in the Marina cracked and crumbled, and fires burst out from broken gas pipes under them; while the skyscrapers built to more modernized codes swayed but stood up. Residents lost power and water. Thousands of commuters were stranded — and some were killed, when a section of the Bay Bridge caved in and feeder freeways collapsed, crushing the people below. The 60,000 baseball fans gathered at Candlestick Park for the aborted World Series felt the venerable stadium shudder, but it and they survived.

Just like San Francisco. And as long as she has citizens with that kind of drive and undefeatable spirit, the City by the Bay will always be able to rise from the ashes.

A cable car gripman uses brute strength to turn the City's movable historic landmark at the Market and Powell Street turnaround. After its direction is changed the unique cable car will make its way down to Victorian Park near the Maritime Museum and Aquatic Park.

At attention: Michael Tilson Thomas leads orchestra and audience in the national anthem at the San Francisco Symphony's season opening.

CULTURE AND THE ARTS

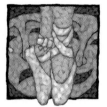

San Francisco is virtually unmatched among major cities in both cultural diversity in, and public support for, the visual and performing arts — and they are an important segment of the local economy, as well. Nearly one in ten employed San Franciscans derives some income from artistic or cultural pursuits, and over 60,000 people are employed in this way.

World-class ballet, symphony, and opera companies are joined by ethnic ensembles and every form of dance troupe. The City's rich theatrical community offers Shakespeare, contemporary, vaudeville, circus, musical comedy, cabaret, political agitprop, multi-media shows, and a wide variety of experimental productions.

The visual arts are represented by permanent collections in six major museums, as well as some 65 ethnic, cultural, and special-focus museums; while corporate and private collections support more than 150 fine-arts galleries and three major fine-arts presses.

The arts industry enjoys strong participation and support, deriving an impressive 50 percent, on average, from box-office receipts. Bay Area corporations give more than $6 million annually to arts and culture organizations through grants, fundraising activities, and encouragement of employee participation. This is not only generous, it is also good business, since the arts community is one of the strongest magnets attracting talented employees to the area.

Many other industries either draw from or contribute to (or both) nonprofit arts organizations, including design, advertising, publishing, film, and the media.

Hundreds of festivals and street fairs help bring the arts into Bay Area neighborhoods each year — just one more element that makes cultural celebration such a vital and exciting part of Bay Area life.

Here are a few of the cultural venues that prove of greatest interest to residents and visitors:

SAN FRANCISCO PUBLIC LIBRARY

This is the largest citizen/government partnership ever undertaken in San Francisco. Following a $109 million bond issue and a $30 million private capital campaign, the City opened a seven-story, 375,000 square-foot new home for one of America's most active public library

San Francisco Ballet; Photographer-Lloyd Englert

Elizabeth Loscavio and Anthony Randazzo perform in Nanna's Lied for the San Francisco Ballet.

San Francisco Convention & Visitors Bureau; Photographer-Frank DiMarco

A San Francisco landmark since the 1915 Panama-Pacific International Exposition, the Palace of Fine Arts was restored in 1967 at a cost of $7.6 million. It now houses the Palace of Arts and Sciences, an "Exploratorium" of science, technology and human perception, and a 1,000-seat theater.

San Francisco Symphony. Photographer–Terrence McCarthy

Michael Tilson Thomas, who became the San Francisco Symphony's Music Director in 1995, is one of the few American-born conductors of any major U.S. orchestra.

systems. The library, with its Beaux Arts exterior designed by James Ingno Freed and Cathy Simon, is the final element in the San Francisco Civic Center, which was originally conceived in 1912 by Daniel Burnham.

FINE ARTS MUSEUMS OF SAN FRANCISCO

The Fine Arts Museums of San Francisco consists of the California Palace of the Legion of Honor, and the M.H. de Young Memorial Museum. Exhibits at the Legion are primarily European — fine and decorative arts from the middle ages to the early 20th century. The collection includes 109 Rodin sculptures, and the Legion is also home to the Achenbach Foundation for Graphic Arts. The principal focus at the de Young is on American work, centered around the distinguished Abby Aldrich Rockefeller Collection. Also displayed at the de Young are the Fine Arts Museums' collections of ancient art works, and the art of Africa, Oceania, and the Americas.

SAN FRANCISCO MUSEUM OF MODERN ART (MOMA)

While building a permanent collection of 14,000 works of modern and contemporary art, MOMA has pioneered the recognition of many new art forms, such as photography, design, film/video, and performance. Today, the Museum's strength lies in early 20th-century modernists of Europe and America; photography; and its unrivaled collection of post-1940 Bay Area artists — displayed in its magnificent new facility designed by Swiss Architect, Mario Botta.

The world-renowned San Francisco Symphony presented its first concerts in 1911, and in 1980 moved into the newly built Davies Symphony Hall.

SAN FRANCISCO BALLET

Founded in 1933, this is the country's oldest professional ballet company, and one of today's three largest and most important. Its long tradition of artistic "firsts" include the first full-length American productions of *Coppelia*, *Swan Lake*, and *The Nutcracker*. Its new $14 million facility provides ample space for the Ballet's 60-member repertory company and the 300 students of the San Francisco Ballet School. The first American ballet company to tour the Far East, the San Francisco Ballet has also made appearances in Europe, Latin America, and the Near East.

SAN FRANCISCO OPERA

Grand Opera has always been an important part of San Francisco's cultural life, and the 3,200-seat War Memorial Opera House is the nation's first municipally-owned opera venue. Since its founding in 1923, the San Francisco Opera has produced 144 operas, premiered 21 full-length operas, and debuted more than 300 singers, directors, conductors, and designers.

SAN FRANCISCO SYMPHONY

One of America's elite orchestras, the San Francisco Symphony has been honored five times in recent years by the American Society of Composers, Authors, and Publishers for adventuresome programming of new music. In 1926, it offered the country's first syndicated radio broadcasts — and today, The Symphony has more than 200 live performances broadcast by some 250 radio stations worldwide. The Symphony has received honors from many nations for its broadcasts, recordings, and tour performances, including the *Grand Prix du Disque* of France, and Belgium's Caecelia Prize. The San Francisco Symphony chorus, one of the world's outstanding choral groups, has been heard on the soundtracks of award-winning films like *Amadeus*. The SFS Youth Orchestra, founded in 1980, has earned the City of Vienna Prize   the world's highest honor for an ensemble of young musicians. The Symphony offers a full 52-week season, which includes 29 weeks of performances in the 3,000-seat Davies Symphony Hall.

San Francisco Ballet's production of Swan Lake with Tina LeBlanc and David Palmer.

SCIENCE MUSEUMS OF SAN FRANCISCO

The California Academy of Sciences, founded in 1853, is the oldest science museum in the western U.S. Located in Golden Gate Park, the museum complex contains one of the world's largest herbaria, a planetarium with Foucault Pendulum, and the Steinhart Aquarium. In addition to its permanent exhibits on science and natural history, the Academy sponsors many scientific expeditions, and related research and publications. The Exploratorium, housed in the Palace of Fine Arts, pioneered the concept of "hands-on" science education for children, featuring lively interactive exhibits and a wide array of science classes for both youngsters and adults.

ASIAN ART MUSEUM OF SAN FRANCISCO

This museum, housed since its founding in a specially-constructed wing of the M.H. de Young Memorial Museum, has now been awarded the old Main Library for its new home, and is due to open in 1999. Thanks to $38 million in city bonds, and $35 million in private capital, the Asian will have four stories and 185,000 square feet in the renovated Beaux Arts palace in which to display the world's most impressive collection of pan-Asian art — the largest outside Asia. The collection's 12,000-plus objects, reflecting 6,000 years of cultural history, include bronzes, jades, ceramics, and lacquers; the oldest known dated Buddha figure (338 AD); and a bronze rhinoceros cast in the 11th century BC.

While San Francisco is, of course, the cultural hub of the region, other Bay Area communities also have a great deal to offer connoisseurs of the arts:

EAST BAY

The City of Walnut Creek in Contra Costa County opened its 72,000 square-foot Regional Center for the Arts in 1991. The Center includes two theaters (the 800-seat Hofmann and the 300-seat Dean Lesher), as well as the Bedford Gallery for contemporary and folk art. Making their permanent homes at the Center are the California Symphony, the Diabolo Light Opera Company, and the Center Repertory Company. In Alameda County, the City of Fremont is planning a $45 million performing arts facility which will also include two theaters and an art gallery; while the Cities of Livermore, Dublin, and Pleasanton have launched a joint effort to create a multi-purpose arts center for the Livermore-Amador Valley.

OAKLAND MUSEUM

The unique park-within-a-museum design of Oakland Museum sprang from the genius of Kevin Roche. The four-square-block structure houses separate museums of art, history, and natural history. The museum exhibits two centuries of California crafts and visual arts, and its fine arts collection is built around 19th-century California landscapes by artists like Thomas Hill and Alfred Bierstadt.

STANFORD UNIVERSITY MUSEUM OF ART

In addition to the previously-mentioned outdoor sculpture-garden collection of Rodin's work, this museum offers a significant collection of Near East and Mediterranean antiquities. It even houses the golden

Designed by Swiss architect Mario Botta, the San Francisco Museum of Modern Art houses over 15,000 artworks representing media arts, design photography, painting and sculpture. The MOMA is located directly across from Center for the Arts at Yerba Buena Gardens, and within walking distance of the Moscone Convention Center, Financial District and Union Square.

Sar Francisco Convention & Visitors Bureau; Photographer-Dawn Stranne

Located on a headland where the Pacific Ocean meets San Francisco Bay, the California Palace of the Legion of Honor is one of the most dramatic museums in the country. It was given to San Franciscans by Mr. and Mrs. Adolph Spreckels on Armistice Day, 1924 to honor Californians who died during World War One.

spike that completed the nation's first transcontinental railroad — appropriate, since Leland Stanford was probably the best known of the infamous "Railroad Barons." Built in 1892, this is the west's oldest art museum.

BERKELEY REPERTORY THEATRE

Founded in 1968, Berkeley Rep is known today for its innovative, and often daring, approach to both new dramatic works and rarely-produced classics. The Rep often works with the international drama community to continue its tradition of translation and adaptation to reflect the modern cultural reality.

SOUTH BAY

The Mountain View Center for the Performing Arts, in Santa Clara County, opened in early 1991 as part of Mountain View's $45 million Civic Center. Center venues include a 625-seat theater, a 200-seat flexible performance space, and a 300-seat outdoor amphitheater, plus support facilities and rehearsal space. San Jose also opened a new arts facility in 1991 — a $14 million, 45,000 square-foot addition to its Museum of Art, which doubled exhibition space.

ETHNIC/CULTURAL ARTS GROUPS

El Teatro de la Esperanza is one of the oldest American theatrical companies dedicated to works drawn from Latin culture, history, and mythology. The resident theater company at San Francisco's Mission Cultural Center, Esperanza has created more than two dozen original works, including contemporary classics like *La Victima* and *Hijos: Once a Family*. It is the nation's only Chicano theater company with a regular touring schedule, and also teaches theater arts through a variety of civic and educational outlets.

Mandeleo Institute, founded in 1974, is an innovative organization devoted to preserving and promoting African cultural arts, music, drumming, dancing, and storytelling. In 1979, the Institute began presenting the annual "African Cultural Festival" — the country's biggest such extravaganza. Other large-scale events sponsored by the nonprofit Institute highlight music, drama, and dance with African or African-American origins.

A REAL WRITER'S TOWN

San Francisco has always embraced writers, beginning with 19th-century novelists like Bret Harte, Frank Norris, and Robert Louis Stevenson (who spent time in San Francisco in the 1880s). Poet and author Jack London was born in The City, and there is a Square named after him in Oakland.

When the 1950's came rolling in, so did the writers of the Beat Generation (including Jack Kerouac, who coined the term). Poets like Allen Ginsberg and Lawrence Ferlinghetti launched the Beat Movement in the Bay Area. They all tended to congregate in the North Beach district, giving it a long-standing reputation as a Bohemian stronghold.

The City has also produced countless great journalists. Among them is their undisputed dean, the venerable Herb Caen — who, through a half-century of newspaper columns (mostly for the San Francisco Chronicle*) and books like* Baghdad By The Bay *and* Don't Call It Frisco*, captured the wonder and beauty of his favorite city as nobody else has ever quite managed to do.*

Authors of the hard-boiled genre of detective stories have long loved to use San Francisco as a setting (Sam Spade and the Maltese Falcon were born here), as have the writers and directors of the film noir *school; and those in the action-adventure category, as well.*

It is a town that has always liked writers, and the affection is mutual. That is why so many literary masterworks were written here, and why there will surely be many more to follow.

San Francisco Ballet's Tina LeBlanc lends grace and elegance to Pacific.

In terms of shipping, the Port of San Francisco has long been the call of choice for containerized trade from Latin America, as well as such traditional breakbulk (non-containerized) shipments as newsprint and Mercedes automobiles.

Port of San Francisco

TRANSPORTATION AND COMMUNICATION

For more than 200 years, San Francisco visionaries have been putting as much time and attention into the development and refinement of their transportation and communications systems as they have into education, research, and invention. Such systems are, of course, essential ingredients in business success — and the Bay Area's can compete with any of the world's best, extending the local economy far beyond state and national borders.

TRANSPORTATION

In addition to the three international airports and nine seaports previously mentioned, the area is served by three Class I railroads and two interstate freeways, while intensive use of mass transit expedites travel within the region.

Air

The three airports serve more than 41 million passengers and transports 3.4 billion pounds of air cargo each year, and are assisted by 25 regional airports. Commercial activities account for 45 percent of all takeoffs and landings at area terminals; the other 55 percent is commuter, military, and general aviation operations. San Francisco International is by far the region's largest, handling 74 percent of passenger traffic and 53 percent of air cargo (mainly international shipments). Oakland International, the area's primary domestic-cargo terminal, is responsible for 44 percent of air cargo. San Francisco International's $2.5 billion expansion will be completed in 1999.

Sea

Ports located on the Bay itself, at San Francisco, Oakland, and Redwood City work together with Richmond on San Pablo Bay, and the ports along the Sacramento River — at Antioch, Benicia, Pittsburg, Sacramento, and Stockton — to handle people, petroleum, freight, and fish. Oakland boasts one of the world's largest container-shipping ports, handling 90 percent of the Bay Area's seaborne trade;

Wyndham Images

For nearly a century, the development of the modern telecommunications industry has been dictated by Bay Area research.

The Port of San Francisco, the City's seven and one-half mile stretch of publicly owned waterfront, supports more than a dozen different industries, both maritime and commercial; provides the ambiance for some of the City's best parties; and is home to one of the country's most popular tourist attractions.

Port of San Francisco

The Cable Car Barn, home for Muni's world-famous cable cars, also houses the Cable Car Museum, one of the world's favorite free tourist attractions.

petroleum and other liquid bulk moves through Richmond; automobiles through Benicia; and agricultural products and commodities are handled by the Ports of Sacramento and Stockton. San Francisco is not only the region's port of call for cruise ships, but is home port for one of California's largest commercial fishing fleets, as well.

Rail

The three Class I railroads in the region — Santa Fe, Southern Pacific, and Union Pacific — serve seven of the Bay Area's seaports, and provide freight transportation throughout the region. Passengers are served by Amtrak, which operates two-way daily service between Seattle and Los Angeles (the Coast Starlight) via the Bay Area, and between here and Chicago (the California Zephyr). Amtrak also carries passengers to and from the Bay Area and San Joaquin in the Central Valley, three times a day.

Road

The Bay Area marks the midpoint of Interstate Highway 5, which traverses the west coast from the Canadian border to the Mexican, covering 1,382 miles. The Area is also the western terminus of Interstate 80, connecting San Francisco with New York, 2,907 miles away. Spurs and beltways of these two, together with regional and local freeways, highways, and major roads, create a surface-transportation grid across the region. Several of these smaller freeways were damaged in the 1989 Loma Prieta earthquake, and are still being redesigned and rebuilt, with large portions being converted from elevated to underground expressways. Traffic flow across the Bay and through the area's hills is facilitated by eight major bridges and eleven tunnels.

Regional Mass Transit

The three major employment centers of the Bay Area — San Francisco, Oakland, and San Jose — rank among the six heaviest users of mass transit in the United States. San Francisco, with nearly a million boardings a day, is second only to New York as the nation's most transit-oriented metropolis. While Bay Area Rapid Transit (BART) is headquartered in Oakland, the system was originally developed to move commuters in and out of San Francisco, which it still does most efficiently. Within the 49 square miles of the City itself, passengers can ride on the San Francisco Municipal Railway (Muni), which actually consists of a light-rail subway (Muni Metro); diesel buses; electric trolley coaches; a collection of historic streetcars; and, of course, the landmark cable cars, beloved by visitors and residents alike.

Commuters, too, have many options. BART's heavy-rail subway system works with a network of express feeder buses, Caltrain Peninsula Commuter Service, and ferry boats (some belonging to the Golden Gate Bridge, Highway, and Transportation District, and some to the privately-owned Red And White Fleet). Several regional bus lines serve the Bay Area, and most of its cities and towns have their own bus services. BART even runs under the Bay — a major engineering and construction feat — and peak commute hours see a high-speed train sent through this tube every two minutes and 15 seconds. AC Transit diesel buses offer additional transport across the Bay Bridge, and provide intracounty service in Alameda and Contra Costa Counties. Bart is now designing extensions — in Contra Costa County, northeast from Concord to Pittsburgh; in Alameda County,

In FY 1996, 31 million domestic passengers and seven million international passengers enplaned and deplaned at San Francisco International Airport.

San Francisco International Airport

The trademark of The Port of San Francisco is the Ferry Building that stands at the Embarcadero. The clock tower is 230 feet high and was modeled by Arthur Page Brown after the campanile of Seville's cathedral. At left is the modern skyscraper of The Embarcadero Center.

east to Dublin and Livermore, and southeast to Warm Springs. Construction has been proposed for a private toll road covering portions of four counties, running northward from San Jose (Santa Clara County) through the eastern parts of Alameda and Contra Costa, and on to Fairfield in Solano County.

Commuter service from the North Bay counties of Marin and Sonoma is provided by the diesel buses and ferries of the Golden Gate Bridge, Highway, and Transportation District, which also offers intracounty bus service in Marin. These two counties are considering options to purchase right-of-way for a light rail system linking their major employment centers, and a transit connection to link them with BART in Contra Costa County via the Richmond Bridge. South Bay communities like San Jose and San Mateo are served by Caltrain, SamTrans, and Santa Clara County Transit District (SCCTD). Intracounty buses and feeder buses join light-rail systems to move commuters around the area. BART is planning to extend its heavy-rail system south to San Francisco International Airport (which is actually in San Mateo County), and the feasibility of more BART extensions in the South Bay is being studied. San Francisco, Santa Clara, and San Mateo Counties have secured State funding to acquire Southern Pacific right-of-way for extension of light-rail service from San Francisco to San Jose via the airport.

COMMUNICATIONS

For nearly a century, the development of the modern telecommunications industry has been dictated by Bay Area research. Inventions like the vacuum tube, the klystron tube, the image-dissector tube, and the microprocessor helped form the foundations of the industry. Transmission facilities include lines, fiber-optic cables, and the most advanced microwave equipment offering direct access to both Atlantic and Pacific satellite networks. Here, in one of the nation's largest and fastest-growing telecommunications markets, the industry is supported by state-of-the-art research facilities, product development and manufacturing, carriers, and regulators.

THE BAY THAT WASN'T THERE

For hundreds of years, explorers representing the world's great naval powers sailed along the California coast. Because of the heavy fogs so common to the region, however, they failed to realize that the narrow strait now known as the Golden Gate led to one of the greatest natural harbors ever discovered. The best evidence suggests that Sir Francis Drake, under the English flag, was the first to enter the bay in 1579. There he found a harbor some 48 miles long, and three to twelve miles wide, of which 70 percent is less than twelve feet deep.

Spain's Portola-Serra expedition of 1769 stumbled across the bay while searching for Monterey Bay. In 1776, when the American Revolution was being launched in the east, Fra Junipero Serra established the mission which would become the first foundation of the City of St. Francis, although the settlement was originally known as Yerba Buena ("Good Herbs" — still the name of the small island across which the Bay Bridge passes).

Muni Metro serves Market Street and shares four downtown stations with BART, the regional rail system, providing easy connections.

These restored Victorians are prime examples of the Stick style popular in the 1880s. All but indistinguishable from Italianate, the Stick style, sometimes referred to as Eastlake, features chamfered corners on pillars, strips, incised decoration, and horseshoe arches.

NATURAL ENVIRONMENT AND QUALITY OF LIFE

Of all the many elements that make the Bay Area such a wonderful place to live, work, and raise a family, and which help local businesses to attract key employees, the closeness to nature enjoyed by area residents has to rank near the top. The varied topology of the region, from wooded hills and coastal mountains to warm valleys and cold Bay waters, produces a micro-climate to suit every taste and lifestyle. All the treasures of the natural world are never far away.

Just a short drive from the cities, one finds the primeval redwood landscape of Muir Woods; the dramatic cliffs, lonely beaches, and tide-pools of Big Sur and the Sonoma Coast; the lush green Sacramento River Delta; the broad fields and orchards of the Great Central Valley; the orderly vineyards of the wine country; and the rugged, snowcapped peaks of the high Sierra. And, in the case of at least one famous park, you do not even have to leave town.

Golden Gate Park

A glorious woodland sanctuary, which stretches from the heart of the City to the shores of the ocean, this beloved park is a testament to the determination, creativity, and hard work of people with a dream — and city government that shared it. Walking, driving or riding through the park today, it is hard to believe that virtually all of it is man-made. Beginning in 1870 with a thousand acres of windswept sand-dunes, the City started its historic reclamation project by anchoring the sand with barley, stabilizing the dunes with deep-rooted lupine, and individually planting thousands of pine, cypress, and eucalyptus trees, to help break the force of the strong westerly winds. Over the past century, the sandy soil has been enriched by constant cultivation, and the mild and often foggy climate has encouraged the original plants, grasses, and trees to spread and flourish. The broad range of horticultural specimens found in the park include many which bloom nowhere else in North America. The Conservatory, modeled after one at Kew Gardens in London, contains many rare hothouse plants. Bike trails and bridle paths make it possible for park-goers to explore this mini-wilderness up close. Attractions like the famed Japanese Tea Gardens, Steinhart Aquarium, and San Francisco's

Photograher-Robert L. Elvin

View north from Point Reyes.

The serene and beautiful Japanese Tea Gardens in Golden Gate Park.

Photographer-Joel Eis

Angel Lake near Donner Pass.

Photographer-Miguel Farias

Zoo make Golden Gate Park the perfect place for family fun. Thanks to the far-seeing dedication of those early San Franciscans, Golden Gate Park has blossomed into a unique natural resource — an international destination for horticulturists, and a weekend jaunt for Bay Area residents. To the locals, though, it is just the back yard.

Golden Gate National Recreation Area

The world's biggest urban park, the GGNRA brings together pastoral, historic, military, public, and city lands, including Point Reyes National Seashore, Muir Woods, Mt. Tamalpais State Park, Angel Island, Alcatraz, and the Presidio in San Francisco; forming a 40-mile-long greenbelt encompassing more than 140,000 acres. The combination of scenic wonders and recreational opportunities makes this America's most popular national park, hosting 25 million visitors each year — four times as many as Yellowstone, Yosemite, and the Grand Canyon combined.

The Presidio

Occupying 1,774 forested acres on the San Francisco headlands, the Presidio has been in continuous operation as a military base since the Spanish founded it in 1776. Recently ceded by the Army to the GGNRA (see above), the Presidio commands breathtaking views of The City, the Bay, the Golden Gate, and the ocean.

Muir Woods

In Marin county, less than ten miles from San Francisco's financial district, lies Muir Woods, a 2,000-year-old redwood forest. A living monument to the great naturalist John Muir, this was the country's only coastal redwood park until 1968.

Henry W. Coe State Park

In contrast with the moist, misty climate of the coastal parks, the 67,000 acres of Henry W. Coe State Park, in Santa Clara County, are exceptionally hot and dry in summer, and offer over 100 miles of uncrowded hiking trails. Open, hilly grasslands support the full range of local dry-land flora and fauna, and the park gives us a rare glimpse of the way all of inland California must have looked before the first European settlements.

East Bay Regional Parks

There are over 60,000 acres in the East Bay Regional Parks District, comprising some 40 parks in Alameda and Contra Costa Counties, eight freshwater lakes, two Bay islands, and more than 1,000 miles of hiking trails. The Skyline Trail, part of the National Trails System, follows the crest of the East Bay hills for 31 miles, from Richmond to Castro Valley.

IT'S NOT ALL PARKS

While parks and watersheds make up the major blocks of public open space in the Bay Area, it is the local landscape itself that brings the people so close to the natural world.

Here, at the very edge of the continent, mountains and cliffs soar abruptly out of the Pacific, beaches scalloping their feet, working with the hills, rivers, bays, and ocean to create the landscape and weather found nowhere else. Westerly winds blow clean, mild air through the environment — and, while summer days can be hot, nightfall almost invariably brings the famous fogs rolling in to cool things off.

The lush winter green of the area testifies that it gets its share of annual rainfall (24 inches in San Francisco), but it is not uncommon to experience warm, sunny days in December.

Another thing which makes this region unique as living space is the way in which the man-made environment harmonizes with the natural. This is what a century or so of caring and study can do — environmental awareness has become so deeply ingrained in the local consciousness as to be almost second nature to those who are lucky enough to live here. The lessons to be learned in how nature, industry, and the population can co-exist without undue strain on any of the parties have been learned well here and are learned anew by all who flock here to be a part of this extraordinary three-way partnership.

MORE WEATHER NOTES

The San Francisco Bay Area, as noted above, enjoys an overall climate that is temperate, with most of the precipitation concentrated in the winter months. Compared with most other places located at Latitude 37 North, the area is relatively cool in summer and warm in winter.

On average, day and night temperatures vary by only 12 degrees, and the same separation is seen between the coldest month (January) and the warmest (September). In a way, it is almost "eternal spring," where flowers bloom all year, and you may need warm clothes in any month. Thousands are discovering that this makes for an ideal climate in which to work and live.

Within the Bay Area itself, there are dramatic differences in climate from place to place — and, in San Francisco, from neighborhood to neighborhood. More or less rain, warmer or cooler, fog or none: there is a microclimate for everyone.

What About The Fog?

From May through August, the great difference between land and sea air-temperature intensifies the prevailing westerly winds, which pull cool marine air in through the Golden Gate and other coastal gaps. Rivers of fog flow into low-lying areas like the Bay, to be burned off with the rising of the sun. San Franciscans are proud of the fog — and it certainly does add an eerie, dreamlike, almost otherworldly atmosphere to the local scene.

San Francisco's natural air condi-tioner — the fog — provides a picturesque show of nature that changes each day as the elements of the sea, sun and wind interact over the skyline and Alcatraz island.

EXPLORING THE ROCK

For 30 years, Alcatraz (a variation on the Spanish word for "pelicans") was the most feared name in the criminal community. Widely known as the harshest and most escape-proof Federal prison in the country, Alcatraz hosted the worst offenders in the U.S. prison system from 1933 to 1963. The fortress-like structure of the prison — and, even more, the icy waters and strong currents of the Bay — forestalled all but a handful of escape attempts, virtually all of which failed. Infamous inmates included gangster boss Al Capone and Robert Stroud, the "Birdman of Alcatraz."

The island was named by the Spanish in 1775, and became a U.S. military reservation in 1850. Civil War prisoners were interned here, and in 1909, it officially became a military prison.

After its closure in 1963, the prison stood empty until 1969, when it was taken over by a group of Native Americans unsuccessfully attempting to win government recognition of their claim to the island. They held it until 1971; and it was then opened to the public in 1972, as part of the Golden Gate National Recreation Area.

Today, this once-fearsome "Rock" is a favorite tourist attraction and souvenir stop, but to those who know its grim history, it will always seem like a slightly sinister blot on the beautiful Bay.

The oldest structure in San Francisco's Golden Gate Park is the Conservatory of Flowers. An import from England, this glorious glass confection was completed in 1879 and is considered the Bay Area's most outstanding example of Victorian architecture.

The nefarious past of Alcatraz, "the Rock," is an irresistible draw for thousands of tourist each year.

San Francisco Bay is no place for amateurs on a gusty day. When the ebb tide's at its crest, the flow through the Golden Gate surpasses that of the Mississippi River at its mouth.

Chapter Ten

SPORTS AND OUTDOOR RECREATION

SPORTS AND OUTDOOR RECREATION

One of the advantages conferred by the Bay Area's temperate climate is the opportunity to enjoy outdoor activities year 'round. With more than 700 parks in the region, public and private venues for exercise and competition abound, while sports fans can cheer for seven pro franchises in five different sports, plus a full roster of collegiate competitors.

For those who would rather do than watch, the Bay Area offers hundreds of miles of scenic hiking trails; dozens of golf courses, public and private (including several championship courses); and of course there are the beaches, offering endless opportunities to swim, fish, sail, and windsurf — or to just bask in the sun, or take a quiet stroll along the tide-line. The area has multitudes of clubs devoted to cycling, striding, walking, and running. More than 500 organized competitive running events, from biathalon to marathon, take place each year (thousands annually turn out for the Bay to Breakers 10K Run, which goes from the Bay shore up the hills through San Francisco, and back down to the Pacific). Soaring and hot-air ballooning have become popular pastimes, especially in the beautiful wine country. Sailing, on the Bay, the rivers, or the many lakes of the region generates widespread enthusiasm, and San Francisco is home port to a very large sport-fishing fleet.

For the truly bold and adventurous, there are organized swims around Alcatraz and across Golden Gate Strait, battling cold waters and stiff currents. Winter sports are never too far away, either, as the deep-snow ski slopes and trails of the Sierras are only a three-hour drive from the Bay Area.

San Francisco Giants

Legendary Hall-of-Famer Willie Mays is one of the San Francisco Giants' most celebrated players of all time.

Thousands participate in the annual Bay to Breakers Run.

San Francisco 49ers; Photographer-Michael Zagaris

Stretching across three miles, Golden Gate Park is a playground for everyone. People can rent a boat at Stow Lake, view the exhibits at the many museums in the park or chew the fat with a herd of buffalo. On Sundays, Martin Luther King Drive is closed to vehicles, allowing bicyclists and in-line skaters to take over the road. Here, two skaters go off the beaten path.

San Francisco Convention & Visitors Bureau; Photographer-Mark Downey

Quarterback Steve Young has led the NFL in passing four times and has twice been named the league's Most Valuable Player.

PROFESSIONAL SPORTS

Fans of almost every kind of professional sport will find plenty to root for in the Bay Area, which boasts pro franchises in football, baseball, basketball, hockey, and soccer. The San Francisco 49ers, considered *the* football team of the 80's, have Superbowl rings from 1982, 85, 89, and 1990. The recent return of the Oakland Raiders from Los Angeles to the town where they were born has sparked new East Bay interest in pro football. The Oakland Athletics (A's) won baseball's World Series in 1989, and the San Francisco Giants captured the 1989 NL Championship. Hoops fans can watch the NBA's Golden State Warriors, who play at Oakland Coliseum Arena; hockey lovers have the San Jose Sharks, playing at the Cow Palace; and the San Francisco Bay Blackhawks keep professional-soccer aficionados at San Jose's Spartan Stadium entertained.

COLLEGE SPORTS

Bay Area colleges and universities participate in NCAA Divisions 1, 2, and 3. Athletes compete in football, basketball, baseball, track, crew, rugby, polo, fencing, swimming, soccer, gymnastics, tennis, and field hockey. While the Division 1 "Big Game" between the Stanford Cardinal and the California Golden Bears of UC Berkeley is the annual highlight of a 100-year-old football rivalry, the Area's reigning collegiate champions are the Cal Aggies of UC Davis, who hold a record of 19 consecutive Division 2 football championships. The Aggies also made a major splash on the polo scene, both men's and women's teams capturing the national title on their maiden efforts in 1975 and 1977, respectively. The men's team now has nine championships to their credit, and the women have five.

The San Francisco Giants' Osvaldo Fernandez is the franchise's bright new pitching prospect.

Chester McGlockton is a force for the Raiders along the defensive line.

Long Photography

BAY AREA PROFESSIONAL SPORTS FRANCHISES

Baseball:
AL - Oakland Athletics (A's)
NL - San Francisco Giants

Football:
NFC - San Francisco 49ers
AFC - Oakland Raiders

Basketball:
Golden State Warriors

Hockey:
San Jose Sharks

Soccer:
San Francisco Bay Blackhawks

FOR RACING FANS

Automobiles:
Sears Point (Sonoma County); Laguna Seca (Monterey)

Thoroughbred Horses:
Bay Meadows (San Mateo); Golden Gate Fields (Albany)

Quarterhorses/Exotic Breeds:
County fairs in Alameda, San Mateo, Solano, and Sonoma Counties.

COLLEGE CONFERENCES

NCAA Division 1
Pac 10
Big West
West Coast

NCAA Division 2
Northern California Athletic Conference

NCAA Division 3
Independent Conference

A young Giants fan takes in a game.

The north tower of the Golden Gate Bridge is silhouetted against San Francisco's glimmering skyline. The towers of the Financial District can be seen to the left in the background.

Part Two

NETWORKS

SAN FRANCISCO INTERNATIONAL AIRPORT

View of SFO's three terminals and airfield.

San Francisco International Airport (SFO) excels at moving passengers and cargo efficiently through its gates and on to other destinations. Due both to the San Francisco Bay Area's economic, cultural, and social ties to Pacific Rim nations and to its location on the West Coast, SFO is heralded as a premier gateway to the Pacific. Of the Airport's 7 million international passengers, 49 percent traveled to and from the Pacific Rim countries, and the most significant growth is expected to occur in this direction. Europe was second with 28 percent, Latin America and the Caribbean accounted for 13 percent, and Canada 10 percent.

San Francisco's Airport is a leader among the world's airports in other ways:

- SFO is second in the U.S. in the dollar value of cargo;
- Nonstop flights originating at SFO go to 63 domestic and 28 international cities;
- SFO's landing fee (what it costs an airplane to land) is the lowest on the Pacific Rim and the second lowest in the U.S.;
- SFO handles 95 percent of the Bay Area's international passenger traffic and virtually all of its international air cargo;
- San Francisco has been rated favorite U.S. city by travelers in seven out of the last eight years in surveys by *Conde Nast Traveler* magazine;
- Throughout its 70-year history, SFO has maintained a sterling safety record;
- In FY 1996, 31 million domestic passengers and seven million international passengers enplaned and deplaned at SFO. These figures represent growth over the previous year of six percent for domestic and 27 percent for international passengers.

"There is a synergy among the nations of the Pacific Rim, San Francisco-based businesses, the high-tech companies of Silicon Valley, the hospitality industry, and San Francisco Airport," says John L. Martin, Airport Director, in explaining this aspect of the growth in traffic.

DIVERSIONS FOR THE TRAVELER
For those who linger a bit, there is much to enjoy in the Airport itself. Many of the shops and restaurants are local businesses, bringing the flavor of the Bay Area right into the Airport. These retail concessions provide welcome convenience for travelers and generate revenue for the Airport and the City of San Francisco.

Reflecting some of the cultural jewels of San Francisco, the Airport is in partnership with the Strybing Arboretum in Golden Gate Park for botanical exhibits and with the Steinhart Aquarium in the California

Computer rendering of the new International Terminal building, opening in Spring 2000.

Academy of Sciences in Golden Gate Park, for the three aquariums on display.

The Airport's Bureau of Exhibitions, Museums, and Cultural Exchange curates over fifty exhibitions a year in the passenger terminals. Its curators collaborate with the Fine Arts Museums of San Francisco to present changing exhibits culled from museums around the world for an audience of over 8,000 people per day in each gallery area. This airport -as-museum program is the first of its kind in the United States.

Exhibits have ranged from Native American baskets to over 200 boomerangs from the South Australian Museum to the Right Foot Show—more than 800 shoes from different parts of the world—to Oscar-winning costumes from *Bram Stoker's Dracula*, the movie directed by Francis Ford Coppola.

THE AIRPORT'S MASTER PLAN — BUILDING FOR THE FUTURE

Over the next ten years, independent aviation experts forecast that total passenger traffic at SFO will increase by 37 percent. Of these passengers, domestic traffic is forecast to increase by 30 percent, international traffic by 76 percent. To accommodate

this tremendous growth, SFO has developed a Master Plan to ensure high service standards for the traveling public into the next millennium.

The centerpiece of the $2.4 billion plan is a new International Terminal that is due to be in service in the spring of the year 2000. At two million square feet, it will be the size of 35 football fields. A grand public hall, with a 65-foot-high ceiling, will accommodate three times the number of passengers checking in than the current building can. It will have special areas designed for tour groups which will eliminate the congestion that can now occur when tour groups gather.

The number of international gates will increase from the current 10 to 26. The new terminal will be able to simultaneously accommodate 21 of the next generation of planes, the larger, wide body aircraft such as the Boeing 747-400. These facilities will allow for the scheduling of more international flights at convenient times and will reduce delays for arriving planes. Baggage claim facilities will simultaneously handle three times the number of flights that they can now.

New Federal Inspection Service facilities will reduce the time it takes to process passengers through Customs and Immigration. The number of

This tunnel runs from SFO's garage to Boarding Area A.

SFO's Control Tower is 150 feet high, and from inside, air traffic controllers can guide one plane taking off or landing every 45 seconds.

SFO's K-9 Division gets high marks for safety — and friendliness, too.

people per hour that the Service can process will rise to 5000 from the current 1200. The average time to get through Customs will decrease to 45 minutes from the present one to two hours.

The new building will be equipped with state-of-the-art security and counter-terrorism systems. Space for restaurants, cafes, and shops will triple.

Other features of the Master Plan include a rapid transit system that will link all the Airport terminals with parking garages and new car rental facilities; a new Bay Area Rapid Transit station; a new airport hotel; and other support facilities. A five-level, centralized car-rental building has been designed that will contain all the car rental agencies and will simplify pickups and drop-offs by having them all at the same location. Approximately 3500 new public parking spaces will be located near the new International Terminal. Roadways will be built to serve the new facilities. The bulk of the passenger facilities is scheduled to be completed by 2001, with most of the Master Plan in place by 2006.

Also in the Plan is a 5000-square-foot Aviation Library and Museum. It will house 10,000 volumes and periodicals on aviation and a collection of artifacts related to the history of commercial air transport and SFO's

role as a gateway to the Pacific. Photographs and memorabilia will be electronically accessible for study and will be used for exhibition programs. The Library and Museum will increase public awareness of the historic achievements of commercial aviation and preserve this history for future generations.

SFO IS AN ECONOMIC ENGINE

SFO is an economic engine for growth throughout the Bay Area. The Airport directly provides over 30,000 jobs to keep itself running now. Construction of the Master Plan provides an additional 3,500 jobs. When the construction is finished, the Airport will have close to 33,500 jobs.

In partnership with the airlines and the hospitality industry, SFO now generates 184,000 jobs in the visitor business, which is the Bay Area's number one industry. When construction is complete, the visitor industry will provide over 190,000 jobs.

Shoppers are pleased with SFO's variety and prices.

Annual business revenue generated by the Airport for Bay Area firms is currently $14.3 billion; after construction it will be $23 billion. Annual tax revenues for federal, state, and local governments are now $2.7 billion; after construction they will total $3.6 billion

GOOD NEIGHBOR POLICY

SFO has encouraged minority- and women-owned businesses to compete for Master Plan and other contract opportunities. To date, minority- and women-owned businesses account for 32 percent of the Master Plan's architectural, engineering, and construction work.

The Airport created two programs to help bring this about. The Surety Bond Program, the first of its kind among airports, helps these businesses obtain bid bonds, payment bonds, and performance bonds to participate in construction work at SFO. The second program is an Owner-Controlled Insurance Program under which the Airport buys general liability, workers compensation, and builders' risk coverage directly from insurance underwriters. Minority- and women-owned businesses often find it difficult to obtain the greater insurance coverage that

this program makes possible. The program also brings insurance costs down for the Airport.

SFO places great importance on being a good neighbor to the communities surrounding it. As part of the Airport's Master Plan Mitigation Program, the Airport has committed up to $120 million in noise insulation funds to neighboring cities. SFO's noise abatement program has succeeded in reducing the number of noise impacted homes by 82 percent since 1980.

As a part of its community service efforts, SFO jointly funds, with San Mateo County and the San Mateo Labor Council, a child care center for airport employees. The Palcare child care center is open twenty hours a day.

The San Francisco International Airport continues in its determination to set the highest standards in safety, service, and convenience for the millions of passengers that travel through its gates each year. Through the implementation of its Master Plan and the continued dedication to community needs, the Airport is well prepared to continue serving the public into the new millennium.

Passengers and visitors can choose from over 40 restaurants, snack bars and cocktail lounges - many with a San Francisco theme.

The Airport's Bureau of Exhibitions, Museums, and Cultural Exchange curates over fifty exhibitions a year, such as this Model Car Exhibit, in the passenger terminals.

KKSF

In a medium that oftentimes rewards the brash and the shocking, one San Francisco radio station makes its mark by emphasizing the soothing sounds it calls "Smooth Jazz."

The unlikely success story of KKSF 103.7 FM began in 1987, when family-owned, Los Angeles based Brown Broadcasting Company purchased a floundering adult-contemporary-formatted radio station. The station's share of listeners between the ages of 25 and 54 earned it a low ranking of 33rd in the country's most crowded and terrain-affected radio market.

The station needed a change. And KKSF was born.

Under the station's new ownership and management team, General Manager David Kendrick and Program Director Steve Feinstein orchestrated a sophisticated blend of contemporary jazz, soft rock and adult-contemporary music. To the marketplace, they promote it as "Music Without Borders."

Featuring artists like Kenny G, David Sanborn and Sting, the station targeted in-office listening during the day, by showcasing these artists in a pleasant, low-commercial environment. At night and on the weekend, the approach was softer to enhance various lifestyle activities.

To compliment the sound, the station's announcers shunned the hype and schmaltz often embraced by radio personalities, instead offering intelligent and insightful commentary regarding KKSF's carefully chosen playlist. Over the years, KKSF announcers have developed strong, one-to-one relationships with listeners both on the air and at events in the community.

KKSF Radio; Photographer-Michael Collopy

Bay Area veteran broadcaster Hoyt Smith has held down the afternoon commute shift on KKSF since the station's inception. He is pictured here in KKSF's new state-of-the-art digital studios in downtown San Francisco.

The revolutionary approach worked. Within a year, KKSF and its new format had catapulted over the competition and moved into the top ten among all stations in the coveted 25-to-54 age group. Since then, the station has consistently garnered rankings in the top three and has been ranked as the number one music station a half dozen times. Eventually, the station's "Music Without Borders" position evolved into what is widely accepted in the industry as the "Smooth Jazz" format.

Employing live announcers 24 hours a day, KKSF relies on radio veterans Roger Coryell, Miranda Wilson, Hoyt Smith, Maria Lopez and Linda Cassidy to host its shows. Weekends bring specialty programming, like a two-hour Saturday show hosted by Bay Area saxophone player Dave Koz. The "Sunday

KKSF Radio; Photographer-Michael Collopy

KKSF has presented checks in excess of $2,000,000 to the San Francisco AIDS Foundation from the proceeds of its Sampler series. Pictured (left to right) Steve Feinstein, KKSF Program Director; Sampler 2 recording Artist, Najee; Pat Christen, Executive Director, SFAF; and KKSF General Manager, David Kendrick.

KKSF's Sampler For AIDS Relief series is one of the largest and most successful fundraising projects of its kind in the country.

KKSF Radio; Photographer-Michael Collopy

"Morning" show eases listeners into the day with peaceful sounds from Enya, Yanni, Vangelis, George Winston and others, while Bay Area Jazz legend Dick Conte spins classic jazz Sunday nights in "The Jazz Cafe."

In addition to the station's commercial success and consistently high ratings, the KKSF staff is justifiably proud of the station's "Sampler for AIDS Relief" series. These eagerly anticipated annual compilation albums, which the station began releasing in 1989, as the AIDS epidemic was reaching crisis proportions in the Bay Area, feature local and international recording artists from KKSF's playlist. Recording industry stars like Bonnie Raitt, Carlos Santana, Randy Crawford and Sting have all donated the rights to the station for their songs.

Over the past seven years, the station has sold more than 350,000 copies of the popular samplers and donated proceeds in excess of $2 million to the San Francisco AIDS Foundation and other Bay Area AIDS services organizations. These funds have been earmarked for AIDS services, education, prevention and advocacy

KKSF has grown, in part, by reaching out to listeners through "relationship marketing." Each year the station hosts several Listener Parties that draw tens of thousands of Smooth Jazz fans. The station's innovative marketing ideas fulfill the original vision, shared by Kendrick and Feinstein, of attracting a large group of musically active adults who would, for all the right reasons, embrace and respond to the station's new format.

Toward that end, KKSF mails out more than 125,000 copies of MusicNotesä™, a quarterly guide to the station's offerings that features record reviews and artist interviews. The station also maintains a fax database of more than 20,000 listeners anxious for music information; programs the BayLineä™, an interactive telephone hotline offering events listings, artist profiles, news, traffic and weather; and sends off Internotesä™, a free electronic magazine e-mailed directly to interested listeners. As befits a radio station in technology-savvy San Francisco, KKSF beat the crowd to the Internet when it become the first commercial radio station in the country to establish a World Wide Web site.

The station makes use of technology in other ways as well. While San Francisco's terrain makes for beautiful views, the area's hills make broadcast-

ing a tricky business for the more than 70 radio stations competing in what probably is the nation's most physically challenging market. KKSF's exceptionally strong signal, which is bolstered by boosters placed throughout the Bay Area, reaches from Santa Rosa in the north to Vacaville in the east and Gilroy in the south.

As federal deregulation begins to affect the radio industry, KKSF stands out as America's highest-rated "Smooth Jazz" station. With the 1996 purchase of the station by the Dallas-based Evergreen Media Corporation pending FCC approval, the hundreds of thousands of Bay Area listeners who have set their dials to 103.7 can continue to expect to hear the smooth jazz sounds that have become such a large part of their lives.

KKSF Radio; Photographer-Michael Collopy

KKSF Artists perform before tens of thousands of listeners a year at free Listener Appreciation concerts. Pictured are Jeff Kashiwa and Russ Freeman of the The Rippingtons, performing in downtown Mountain View.

PORT OF SAN FRANCISCO

The best-known spot on the waterfront is Fisherman's Wharf, which, together with its shopping-emporium neighbor Pier 39, attracts 12 million visitors each year.

There is a seven and one-half mile stretch of land in San Francisco that supports more than a dozen different industries, both maritime and commercial; provides the ambiance for some of the City's best parties; and is home to one of the country's most popular tourist attractions. It is the City's publicly owned waterfront—the Port of San Francisco.

Extending from Aquatic Park to the northern edge of the Hunter's Point shipyard, the Port of San Francisco is the longest continuous port in the world. The businesses on Port property range from restaurants to ship repair, from fish processing to a foreign trade zone. On

any given day, tourists on their way to a sidewalk crab stand at Fisherman's Wharf might pass a crew shooting a Hollywood film (*The Rock* and Eddie Murphy's *Metro* are recent examples) on one side of the street and a crew unloading a shipment of newspaper print on the other.

Undoubtedly the best known spot on the waterfront is Fisherman's Wharf, which, together with its shopping-emporium neighbor Pier 39, attracts 12 million visitors each year. Its phenomenal popularity makes it the third largest tourist attraction in the country, behind only Disneyland and Disney World. In addition to a plethora of restaurants and shops, the area features several unique maritime attractions, including UnderWater World, an adventure aquarium that employs virtual reality to give visitors the sights, sounds, and scents of a plunge deep into the Bay; the beautiful and little-known Fisherman's and Seaman's

The tourist draw to San Francisco's publicly-owned waterfront is easy to understand, considering beautiful scenes such as this one of the Bay Bridge from the Embarcadero.

Memorial Chapel, whose walls bear plaques with the names of those who lost their lives at sea; the World War II-vintage submarine *USS Pampanito*, open for display to more than 250,000 visitors each year; and the *Jeremiah O'Brien*, a World War Two Liberty ship located at Piers 30 and 32.

Its popularity among tourists notwithstanding, most of the Port's activity is dedicated to maritime business. Its recently renovated fish-processing center at Pier 45, which handles 40 million pounds of fish a year, is recognized as the best in the west. With its seismic upgrade and new wastewater system, the facility is a model for others throughout the country.

The Port also boasts the second largest floating drydock on the West Coast of the Americas. When the 836-foot-long container ship *Chance* ran into trouble 1,200 miles off the California coast last winter, it was the San Francisco Drydock Company, operating out of the Port of San Francisco, that helped bring the big ship in and performed the massive repair work.

In terms of shipping, the Port has long been the call of choice for containerized trade from Latin America, as well as

The Port serves 2.2 million ferry passengers and 62,000 cruise passengers a year.

such traditional breakbulk (non-containerized) shipments as newsprint and Mercedes automobiles. It has now begun to add project moves as well, such as the 2,000 tons of machinery needed to set up Toyota's first auto plant in Brazil.

The Port also serves 2.2 million ferry passengers and 62,000 cruise passengers a year. San Francisco is a favored stopping point for cruise ships, especially for the increasingly popular Alaskan market. Ferries arrive at the Port from all around the Bay Area, including Sausalito, Tiburon, Vallejo, and Oakland. Excursion cruises and sport fishing boats complete the bustling picture.

In addition to its appeal for tourists and businesses, the Port's special events and a rejuvenated waterfront have helped to lure local residents down to the water's edge. Some of the City's biggest parties—including the Bill Graham New Year's Eve bash and the San Francisco Symphony's Black and White Ball—are held here, as is the spectacular Fourth of July festival that lights up the sky with the West Coast's biggest fireworks show. The range of other special events going on year-round reflects the diversity of the City itself: the Vietnamese Water Puppets, Viva Mexico, Festa Italiana, the Philippine Independence Day Celebration, and much more. Of course, the Port is the place to be every fall, when San Francisco hosts Fleet Week, a five-day program of ship tours, social events, and breathtaking air shows.

As a part of City government, the Port is overseen by an executive director and the five-member Port Commission, whose members are appointed by the Mayor to serve four-year terms. Unlike most City agencies, however, the Port operates a self-sufficient enterprise agency, receiving no money from the general fund and generating about $32 million a year in revenue.

After an extensive planning process lasting several years, a new Waterfront Land Use Plan has been drafted to help guide the Port's future. Once certified, this plan will open the door for an exciting array of new projects. At the top of the list is the restoration of the hundred-year-old Ferry Building, one of the City's most famous landmarks.

The City's first public boat launch is also planned, along with new ferry berths and improvements to the cruise terminal. While the Land Use Plan stipulates that two-thirds of the Port's property be reserved for maritime uses, it also calls for a diverse range of development for public use and enjoyment as well: public markets, conference facilities, stores, museums, and restaurants.

A working port that also knows how to have a good time, the Port of San Francisco has proven to its residents, business clients, and visitors that, in this case at least, it is possible to be all things to all people.

South Beach Marina is one of the many businesses located in the longest continuous port in the world.

BART

As BART, shorthand for San Francisco Bay Area Rapid Transit District, approaches its 25th birthday—25 years since its gleaming silver doors opened to customers in 1972—it celebrated a birth of another kind. In the summer of 1996, a baby was born on a Fremont Line train, a first for BART. Ever prepared to meet new challenges, BART personnel arranged for a medical team to meet the mother and child when the train reached the Hayward Station. The baby was given a lifetime pass to ride the system for free.

A BART train pulls into the Colma Station platform.

PUTTING THE FUTURE ON TRACK

BART links the Bay Area with a first-class regional rapid rail system that is convenient, economical, pollution-free, and user-friendly. Its 81 miles of double track and 37 stations serve over 70 million riders annually, and it is growing. A new station opened in late 1995 and two more in 1996, with a totally new line with two stations due to open in 1997, when construction also should begin on the extension of BART to the San Francisco International Airport. In addition, BART is protecting the public's investment in the original system through a multi-year, billion-dollar systemwide renovation program.

The first system of its type in the United States to be accessible to people with disabilities, BART is justifiably proud of its record of serving all people. For those who cannot use regular train and bus service, lift-equipped vans and sedans are available for door-to-door service through a partnership with AC Transit and other transit systems in the Bay Area.

KEEPING BART STATE OF THE ART

When BART opened in 1972, it was the most high-tech urban transit system in the world, and has served as the model for every rapid rail system built in the United States since then.

The Transbay Tube that connects San Francisco and the Peninsula with the East Bay is a modern engineering marvel.

The Pittsburg/Bay Point BART Station, opened in December 1996, spans Highway 4, linking the station to a parking lot with space for over 2,000 vehicles.

When it was completed it was the longest underwater transportation tube in the world, 3.6 miles of tubular steel and reinforced concrete resting in a trench of mud as much as 135 feet beneath the surface of the Bay. When the Bay Bridge was closed following the Loma Prieta earthquake in 1989, the tube was the transportation lifeline connecting both sides of the Bay.

Known around the globe for its cutting-edge technology, BART continues to pioneer. A fiber optics cable network running along the BART trackway will provide high-speed information transmission for a new BART communications system. Commercial communications companies will also use the net-work, thus generating new revenues for the publicly-owned system. BART also has broken new high-tech ground by becoming the first transit system in the United States to receive a defense conversion grant from the federal government which is adapting Desert Storm-tested technology to vastly increase the number of trains operated by BART—almost the equivalent of another Transbay Tube. With the accent on the all-electric commute, BART plans to feature electric station cars for work and home trips.

Dynamic, innovative, and customer driven, BART is a major player in providing swift mobility and making the Bay Area such a great place to get around.

The North Concord/Martinez BART Station opened in December 1995 becoming the first new BART station to be added to the system in nearly twenty years.

Celebrating the opening of the Colma BART Station are (left to right) Congressman Tom Lantos, U.S. Secretary of Transportation Frederico Peña, San Mateo County Supervisor Tom Huening, BART Board President Dan Richard and BART Board Vice President Margaret K. Pryor.

SPRINT

The Sprint network is managed by the Network Operations Center (NOC) located in Overland Park, Kansas. The NOC provides a centralized management and control point for the Sprint network which includes switched, packet switched, private line, video conference and international offerings.

Sprint's claim to fame — as anyone who has seen the company's successful advertisements featuring actor Candice Bergen knows — is the nationwide network of fiber-optic cables that offers the company's customers unsurpassed clarity.

Besides its ability to connect far-flung friends through this up-to-date, all-digital medium, the technology-driven telecommunications company also offers businesses — from multinational corporations to the small, entrepreneurial startups that could become tomorrow's industry leaders — a wide range of products and services. The

Sprint Business Services Group offers a combination of voice-, data- and video-transport services that can help businesses of all sizes increase their performance, profitability and productivity so they can better compete in today's global economy.

Bandwidth is the buzzword of the growing computer and multimedia industries that provide the Bay Area with much of its commercial muscle. With an eye to the future, Sprint is participating in a conglomerate that is stringing undersea, fiber-optic cables in an effort to hard-wire the world and offer economical access to increased bandwidth.

In the 1990s, Sprint made several moves that solidified its place in the global telecommunications industry. It inked a partnership deal with Deutsche Telekom and France Telecom — the second- and fourth-largest telephone companies in the world — to form Global One, a new venture that offers business, consumer and carrier markets seamless, global telecommunications.

Closer to home, Sprint has hammered out deals with Mexico's largest telecommunications carrier, Telefonos de Mexico (Telmex), and Call-Net Enterprises Inc., Canada's largest alternative communications provider. These agreements extend Sprint's reach throughout North America.

These and other investments in infrastructure have paid off. Currently, through its extensive relationships with Internet service providers, Sprint carries 60 percent of the international and 40 percent of the U.S. Internet traffic.

To keep its competitive edge, the company maintains engineering facilities in both San Mateo and Kansas City, Missouri. Sprint's Applied Technology Laboratory in Burlingame boasts the bandwidth necessary to test new applications over various kinds of technology.

But the company that started out as a local telephone company in 1899 has not forgotten its roots. Sprint expects its employees to work within their individual communities, and each year, many of the company's 50,000 employees take advantage of paid time off in order to volunteer on projects like the March of Dimes, Project Open Hand and others.

With its high-tech history and its digital infrastructure in place, Sprint is extending its hand to the rest of the world as well.

Muni

Public transit has been a part of San Francisco's cosmopolitan character since the first stage-coach-style vehicles, called "omnibuses," rolled through the city's streets in 1851. Today, the San Francisco Municipal Railway (popularly known as Muni) boasts a fleet of 1,000 buses, street cars and cable cars. During peak travel periods, 700 of these vehicles carry approximately 700,000 passengers on 79 lines each day — a ridership equivalent to the entire population of San Francisco. In this transit-intensive city—only New York City surpasses San Francisco in the percentage of commuters who choose to use public transit—more than 95 percent of the city's addresses are within two blocks of one of Muni's 5,300 stops. San Francisco's historic cable cars, probably the nation's most enduring and nostalgic vision of public transit, are the highlight of Muni service to many passengers.

In 1995, Muni began operating its popular F Market streetcar line. These multi-colored, historic street cars, painted in the colors of the U.S. cities that once used them, currently run up and down Market Street, from Castro Street to the Embarcadero. Construction has already begun on an extension that will take the F line along the waterfront to Fisherman's Wharf by the turn of the century.

Further improvements to Muni's service include the massive Muni Metro Turnback and Muni Metro Extension projects, which will service the city's booming South Beach area and will ease rush-hour slowdowns in the Muni Metro Subway. A planned light-rail line along the Third Street/Bayshore corridor, which was undergoing environmental review in late 1996, should help revitalize the Bayshore and Hunter's Point neighborhoods. All these undertakings are aimed at expanding

Muni provides service to many of San Francisco's breathtaking destinations and views, including Fort Point and the Golden Gate Bridge.

Muni to better serve its ever broadening ridership in the new millennium.

San Francisco residents can purchase a monthly Fast Pass, which offers unlimited usage of Muni's services (and of BART and CalTrain within city limits). Tourists and locals alike will find Municipal Railway PASS-PORTS—available in one-, three-, and seven-day versions, each offering unlimited use of all regularly scheduled Muni vehicles—to be a convenient and inexpensive way to get around in the city. PASSPORTS also offer discounts to select tourist attractions throughout the city.

Muni's energy-efficient street-cars and trolley buses, which run on electricity from San Francisco's Hetch Hetchy Water & Power System, remain a low-cost and environmentally friendly alternative to driving a car. This proves that Muni, one of the first publicly owned transit systems in the country, continues to provide excellent transit to its many riders eight decades after its establishment in 1912!

Shown above is one of Muni's brand new light rail vehicles manufactured by Breda Costruzioni of Pistoia, Italy, and assembled at Pier 80 in San Franicsco.

*Leaving San Francisco under an apricot
eiderdown, a cargoliner sails into the
sunset through the Golden Gate.*

Part Two

BUSINESS AND PROFESSIONS

ORRICK, HERRINGTON & SUTCLIFFE LLP

Orrick, Herrington & Sutcliffe LLP, Photographer-Maggie Heinzel-Neel

Orrick continues its pattern of dynamic growth, in 1996 adding six new leading real estate partners. Pictured are top left to right: Michael Liever, David Fries and bottom left to right: William Murray, Noel Nellis.

There is no mistaking the offices of the law firm of Orrick, Herrington & Sutcliffe LLP, located at 400 Sansome Street in San Francisco. A far cry from the concrete and glass that make up much of the city's corporate landscape, here one encounters an imposing facade of Sierra white granite and a row of monumental pillars capped with federal eagles. Inside, an elevator paneled in solid walnut and bronze takes visitors to the firm's offices.

A DISTINGUISHED HISTORY

This is a particularly fitting choice of locale because Orrick, Herrington & Sutcliffe LLP has a distinguished history as the city's premier finance law firm. The stately, historic building Orrick now occupies is the former home of the Federal Reserve Bank of San Francisco.

It also is fitting that Orrick should make its home in a San Francisco landmark. The firm has been instrumental in some of the most significant events in San Francisco's history. Orrick traces its origins back to 1863, when a predecessor firm was organized to represent the San Francisco Bank, now part of Wells Fargo. Transamerica is another company that has been a client for more than a century.

Orrick also is credited with helping to assemble Pacific Gas & Electric Company and helping to reorganize Fireman's Fund Insurance after the devastating 1906 earthquake and fire. As a pioneer in public financing and municipal bonds, Orrick has also guided the financing of such Northern California landmarks as the Golden Gate and Bay Bridges, BART, the Moscone Center, 3 Com Park and the Oakland Coliseum.

Indicative of Orrick's continuing preeminence in the world of finance, the most recent survey conducted by The American Lawyer ranked it first among all law firms in the country in both asset-backed finance and municipal finance. Orrick also was ranked among the top ten law firms in project finance.

TODAY: A MULTINATIONAL, MULTIDISCIPLINARY FIRM

In the last three decades, without reducing its commitment to the finance practices that formed the cornerstone of the firm's first century of success, Orrick has significantly expanded the scope of its business. In its San Francisco office alone, Orrick employs over 400 people. Since 1986, Orrick has expanded from 200 to more than 375 lawyers, including more than 150 lawyers in San Francisco and Menlo Park. In an era that has not been kind to many law firms, Orrick's financial condition has improved steadily each year. Drawing on its deep roots in the financial markets, Orrick has successfully

Orrick, Herrington & Sutcliffe LLP, Photographer- Richard Sexton

The Banking Hall at Orrick's downtown offices.

Orrick, Herrington & Sutcliffe LLP Chairman and CEO, San Francisco native Ralph H. Baxter, Jr.

managed its growth into new areas and established itself as a multinational and multidisciplinary firm of the future. The firm's recent growth in the areas of employment law, intellectual property, especially within the fast-paced high-tech industry, and its specialization in some of the more complex and involved types of financial transactions are well matched with the focused, intense commitment of Orrick's legal personnel.

The man who has overseen much of Orrick's growth in recent years, and who was largely responsible for designing and building the firm's employment practice (taking it from two lawyers to fifty), is San Francisco native Ralph Baxter. Baxter has been with the firm since the mid-1970s and has been its Chairman and CEO since 1989. The significant expansion of the New York, Washington, and Los Angles offices and the opening

of offices in Singapore and Silicon Valley have occurred during his tenure. He has also overseen restructuring of the firm's management, including development of a management team of lawyers and a strong professional staff, which has freed Orrick attorneys to give their greater attention to client work.

Dean Criddle, Partner in Charge of the San Francisco office and a member of the firm since 1976, notes that Orrick always has "consisted of lawyers who are very intense about the practice of law, enjoy what they

do, and work on it very long and very hard. That's no less true today than it ever was. If anything, we're becoming more like ourselves."

Orrick now has offices in Los Angeles, New York, Sacramento, Silicon Valley, and Washington, D.C., as well as a small but rapidly growing practice in Singapore. The firm is becoming increasingly global. As Chairman and CEO Ralph Baxter explains, "Our roots are in San Francisco, and those roots are an important part of who we are, but today we are truly a global firm."

San Francisco's Old Federal Reserve Bank Building is a fitting choice of locale for Orrick, Herrington & Sutcliffe which has a distinguished history as California's, and perhaps the country's, premier finance law firm.

Orrick's explicit strategy in recent years has been to nurture its core values while stimulating progress. In response to the numerous patent and trademark disputes that are an inevitable feature of the high-tech landscape of Silicon Valley, Orrick has developed a strong intellectual property practice. The firm also has expertise in real estate, environmental and energy law, commodity futures, and governmental affairs. As employment and workplace laws have become increasingly complex and litigious, Orrick has answered the challenge and now boasts a nationally prominent employment practice, representing many of California's most prominent companies in "big-ticket" employment disputes. Dean Criddle points out, "Companies tend to turn to us when they have the most significant employment matters."

The renovation of the Old Fed, Orrick's San Francisco offices, has made the building one of San Francisco's historic landmarks.

Orrick, Herrington & Sutcliffe LLP; Photographer- Richard Sexton

Orrick's central practice areas also are strongly represented in its three other California offices. In Los Angeles, where the firm has 52 lawyers, Orrick has built a strong commercial and securities litigation practice. Orrick lawyers have participated in financing numerous high-profile projects in the Los Angeles area, including the Rose Bowl, the Los Angeles Coliseum, and the Long Beach Aquarium. Sacramento has been a key location for the firm's public finance work and its representation of some of the world's leading companies in California litigation. The Menlo Park office has handled a number of highly visible intellectual property disputes for some of the world's most prominent high-tech companies.

Not surprisingly, it was Orrick's strong financial practice that facilitated the decision to open a New York office in 1984, beginning with six attorneys. Responding to the constricting bond market of the mid-1980s, Orrick elected to expand and solidify its public finance practice in New York. The decision proved to be a wise one.

Orrick, Herrington & Sutcliffe LLP

The old Federal Reserve vault still stands as a symbol of security and safety as Orrick handles some of the most complex financial transactions and high stakes technology and employment litigation for some of the world's leading corporations and organizations.

"We are now among the fastest-growing firms in Manhattan," notes Baxter, "with more than 130 lawyers representing, in one capacity or another, most of the major Wall Street companies in financial matters." In 1992, Orrick also established a Washington D.C. office, which now includes 12 lawyers who work primarily on financial transactions. This gives Orrick a bicoastal presence in the financial markets unmatched by other West Coast law firms.

The decor in the Orrick office building reflects the firm's persona — a solid history combined with state-of-the-art expertise.

TAKING A FIRMWIDE PERSPECTIVE

With its several areas of specialization and its offices around the country, Orrick offers clients a level of service that is more than the sum of its parts. Ralph Baxter points out that "130 years of history is terrific, but if that 130 years of accumulated experience, resources, and knowledge remains in disconnected pieces, we wouldn't be providing clients with the value of our experience. At Orrick, we all have our own approach and specialty, but by taking a firmwide perspective we can more efficiently address our clients' needs."

Part of Orrick's firmwide perspective is a corporate culture that emphasizes teamwork, flexibility, and collegiality. The project financing for a pipeline, for example, might involve a team of lawyers from the San Francisco, New York, and Singapore offices. Or San Francisco and New York attorneys might pool their resources on a complex real estate transaction, combining the strengths of both coasts. "With our approach, we're able to put the best people wherever they're needed," Baxter says.

LOCAL COMMITMENT

In addition to the firm's long-time San Francisco presence and its role in making many of San Francisco's landmarks possible, Orrick is committed to meeting the more personal needs of the community as well. The firm's staff and attorneys are regular participants in such events as the AIDS Walk; Christmas in April (a hands-on project in which volunteers renovate and repair a local low-income home); annual beach cleanups and clothing drives; and the Adopt an Angel program, for which Orrick "adopts" fifty children each Christmas.

"What's really nice about our [charitable] activities," notes Lee Sullivan Elliott, Administrator of the San Francisco office, "is that it isn't one person directing these activities and trying to convince people to sign up. A lot of these are run by the people in the office, so our people are really enthusiastic." The annual United Way drive has yielded some particularly imaginative fund-raising activities: a miniature golf course set up in the office hallways; tricycle races in the historic marble-tiled banking hall; and a dunk tank that put CEO Ralph Baxter—in suit and tie—in the wet seat.

Orrick attorneys and staff also serve the community by logging thousands of pro bono hours each year. Two important recent cases involved advocating for a disabled boy's right to have day care, and working to protect the privacy of young people involved in juvenile court proceedings. Orrick's commitment to its pro bono practice was further underscored in 1996, when the San Francisco Lawyers' Committee for Civil Rights awarded the Robert G. Sproul Jr. Award to San Francisco partner Bill Alderman for his outstanding twenty-year commitment to pro bono legal work in the Bay Area.

THEME FOR THE FUTURE

The blueprint for Orrick's future might best be summed up by the theme for last year's firmwide partners conference: "Built to Last." The firm's intent is to continue pursuing the course that has proven successful thus far—preserving its core and stimulating the kind of change that is needed to compete effectively in the global marketplace.

In its distinguished history and its commitment to meeting the needs of the future, Orrick resembles the city in which it began and still calls home. "We're a lot like San Francisco itself," Baxter remarks. "There's a rich, deep history here, but also a global focus."

Orrick, Herrington & Sutcliffe LLP San Francisco Managing Partner Dean E. Criddle.

CALIFORNIA STATE AUTOMOBILE ASSOCIATION

California State Automobile Association

The yellow tow truck is a familiar— and welcome—sight to AAA members.

Long before San Franciscans searched city streets for elusive parking spaces, there was a time when different automobile-related battles took place. In the early years of this century, when many Californians objected to the cantankerous contraptions, a group of visionary car owners formed an association that dedicated itself to good roads, fair laws and service for motorists.

They called the organization the California State Automobile Association. While early efforts concentrated on road building, sign posting and fighting unfair traffic laws, today CSAA is known for providing peace of mind and security to its 3.7 million members and the public.

While the size of the CSAA's present membership makes it the second-largest chapter of the American Automobile Association (second only to its sister to the south, the Automobile Club of Southern California), the CSAA got off to a much smaller start. Several California automobile clubs — groups of motorists who rallied around the newly available "horseless carriages" at the dawn of the 20th century — merged to form the CSAA in 1907.

When it began, the association had to deal with a public that largely considered automo-

biles to be dangerous, noisy nuisances. CSAA's leaders saw something else: mobility and opportunity. Over the years, their efforts to promote good roads helped transform California's muddy, rutted roads into the efficient and modern thoroughfares travelers enjoy today.

Perhaps the best-known of the CSAA's many member services is Emergency Road Service, which directs tow trucks to stranded drivers. This popular offering got its start in the early 1920s, when the association stationed two tow cars on the hilly byways leading into Yosemite National Park. Vacationers visiting the scenic spot in their automobiles often experienced mechanical problems, and the association provided help. A summer office, offering motoring information and assistance to all Yosemite visitors, also was opened, and another truck was stationed on the stretch of road linking Lake Tahoe and Placerville.

California State Automobile Association

Before AAA, road service usually involved a willing farmer, a strong team, and the exchange of a few dollars.

Following the success of the Yosemite and Lake Tahoe programs, and an extensive analysis of roadside-assistance and towing services offered by AAA-affiliated motoring clubs in the East, the CSAA decided to expand its Emergency Road Service Program to encompass all of its Northern California territory. Today, the emergency-response service shines as one of CSAA's most enduring triumphs, with the association answering over two million member calls per year and dispatching trucks via a computer-aided system.

Another long-standing CSAA tradition, the publication of up-to-date road maps, found CSAA members logging mileage on Bay Area roads during the organization's formative years. The quality of the association's cartographic work was acknowledged when its maps were used to guide dignitaries visiting California, and army recruits headed for West Coast bases during World War II.

As a public service, the association also posted warning and directional signs throughout the Bay Area and the rest of Northern California. The association's street and highway signing department grew along with the automobile and, by 1917, the diamond-shaped yellow road signs posted by the CSAA throughout Northern California had become a vital source of information for all motorists.

"Our yellow sign stands out on the highway like a lighthouse at sea," said the association's president, Percy Towne, at the time. "It is not beautiful or artistic, perhaps, but it is the most reassuring comforter to the traveler ever devised."

The signs posted certainly helped motorists explore the charming California countryside. Unfortunately, those who chose to leave the confines of the city often learned about a new development in local fundraising: speed traps. To protect motorists' rights, the association turned its attention to the rural governments tapping into this new source of revenue. Increased understanding of the benefits of mobility led to better laws, and the end result was a less painful outing for the average motorist.

Early on, CSAA's leaders realized that good roads would be necessary for the widespread adoption of the automobile into American culture. As the association's membership grew, the organization supported statewide measures aimed at expanding California's highway system.

Road service then and now: AAA has been changing tires for many years; now, as shown at top, trucks are dispatched to aid members using the latest telecommunications equipment.

AAA technicians test cars to ensure peak performance.

After voters approved the Golden State's first bond issue for highway construction in 1912, state highway commissioner Burton Towne (who later went on to sit on the CSAA board and serve as the association's president) broke ground on the state's new highway system, starting with the El Camino Real in San Mateo.

Later, the association would champion gas-tax bills and other legislation that assured California's highway system would grow, and grow safely. Over the years, the CSAA supported a variety of measures that helped build the United States' transcontinental highway system.

AAA was the official sign-posting agency in northern California for the first half of the 20th century; here AAA engineers post a warning sign on what would become one of California's best-known landmarks: the Golden Gate Bridge.

The CSAA also entered the insurance business when both it and the automobile itself were young. In 1914, CSAA's second president, P.J. Walker, spoke with many of the nation's auto insurers. Auto insurance policy premiums were uniformly costly at the time, and Walker hoped to gain rate reductions for CSAA's members. Arguing that the club's members were inclined to drive more safely than the population at large, Walker pressed the insurers for rate relief. When those efforts proved unsuccessful, Walker announced that the association would enter the insurance business to protect its members.

Within months, the CSAA Inter-Insurance Bureau was writing policies for its members at rates 30 percent lower than those available through outside insurance companies. Today, the not-for-profit CSAA Inter-Insurance Bureau is the largest insurer of private passenger cars in northern California.

While undertaking these and similar projects, the association has continually grown, and expanded the territory it serves. The club began building its home office in 1925. Even during the Depression, which brought with it a downturn in the CSAA's membership rolls, the association opened new offices in Palo Alto and Monterey. In 1933, CSAA lifted territorial limits on members' Emergency Road Service benefits.

The CSAA's reach also extended eastward. The organization opened its Nevada Division and an office in Reno, Nevada, during the Depression. Today, Utah also is part of CSAA territory.

As the automobile itself has evolved, so has CSAA. Throughout its history, the association always has placed its members' needs first. After spending two decades keeping pace with the changes of the high-growth period that started in the mid-1960s, the association began reassessing its operations in the 1980s.

In these high-tech times, scientific and industrial innovations continually change the ways in which we handle our day-to-day activities. Digital communication and satellite technologies have enabled the development of onboard navigation systems, called global positioning systems, that soon will be standard equipment in autos.

The microchip revolution has imbued cars with a healthy dose of computing power.

While reinventing the organization for these dramatic times, CSAA's leaders have asked the question, "What do the members need?" The answers continue to drive the evolution of the association.

Today, the CSAA focuses on providing information for travelers, security and peace of mind for drivers on the road, and protection against the unforeseen. To that end, the association is developing new ways of disseminating information and providing assistance. Its revved-up World Wide Web site already offers those in the online community travel news and automo-

AAA sponsored School Safety Patrols have helped students protect their classmates since 1922.

bile services. Motorland, the association magazine that started out as California Motorist in 1917, has evolved into a splashy, four-color affair. Also, the CSAA's full-service travel agency books flights, makes hotel and motel reservations, and helps members plan vacations around the world.

The association also is formulating special safety programs for novice and senior drivers. Currently, the association is working on driver-education programs, from developing a curriculum aimed at successfully instilling safe-driving attitudes and values in children, to securing funding for education, to tying the package together with

creative legislation that could provide incentives for young drivers to put safety first when they get behind the wheel.

The challenge facing the "pro-member" CSAA today lies in meeting member needs for auto, travel and a host of other services. As CSAA approaches its centennial anniversary, the historic "motorist's champion" that helped get California roads built and fought for drivers rights is evolving to meet changing member needs in the 21st century.

AAA's free road service often had members up and running without need for a tow.

METROPOLITAN LIFE INSURANCE COMPANY

Conference held at the U.S. Chamber of Commerce, in 1994, to release The Metropolitan Life Survey of the American Teacher: Violence In America's Public Schools, and to award the winners of the Metropolitan Life Foundation "Positive Choices" program. Pictured on the left is Humphrey Taylor, Chairman and CEO, Louis Harris & Associates; on the right is Harry P. Kamen, Chairman, President and Chief Executive Officer, Metropolitan Life Insurance Company.

Insurance is security.

When shopping for the peace of mind that only insurance can bring, it makes sense to go with a known quantity, a company that has built a longstanding reputation for fair dealing, integrity and ethical behavior. The Metropolitan Life Insurance Company is that kind of organization.

Founded in 1868, the Company has a long history of providing complete customer service and satisfaction. MetLife's motto is a simple one, to be the leader in helping people become financially secure, and it reflects the Company's desire to serve its customers. After all, MetLife is a mutual life insurance company; it is co-owned by its policy holders.

The Company's Northern California region, which stretches from the state's northern border south to Monterey and from Hawaii to the eastern edge of Nevada, has grown into one of MetLife's leading regions. Eleven agency offices and approximately 250 MetLife representatives fall under the jurisdiction of the Company's regional headquarters in downtown Walnut Creek.

Happily, MetLife's Bay Area operations reflect the ethnic diversity of the region. For instance, a mostly Vietnamese MetLife agency in San Jose, while marketing to anyone, exists primarily to serve the needs of the South Bay's Vietnamese community. In San Francisco, MetLife plans to expand its operations in order to address the needs of the city's large Chinese community.

The Northern California region, and the Bay Area in particular, epitomizes MetLife's operations. MetLife is a people-oriented company, devoted to doing whatever it can to better serve its customers, and to attract potential customers.

Another fundamental MetLife belief is that giving back to America is a smart, and even economically savvy, move. In order to solidify its status as a solid corporate citizen,

MetLife has always engaged in a wide variety of civic-minded endeavors.

The Metropolitan Life Foundation offers scholarships. The Company sponsors anti-violence campaigns. "The Metropolitan Life Survey of the American Teacher" helps educators identify strengths and weaknesses within the country's public school system. MetLife agencies are encouraged to become involved in the affairs of the communities within which they operate.

MetLife also supports a medical department charged with providing the public with education on fitness and general well-being. Throughout the Company's history, the medical department has conducted research on diseases like tuberculosis and diphtheria and published educational volumes addressing hygiene and similar subjects. In 1925, MetLife even went as far as broadcasting a morning exercise program, described as "the world's biggest gym class" in company literature, from the Metropolitan Tower in New York City.

Historically, MetLife has proven itself to be an insurance company with a heart. During the 1890s, the Company offered to honor the policies of customers whose payments had lapsed as a direct result of having lost their jobs during an economic downturn. In 1906, when San Francisco was devastated by an earthquake and the ravaging fires that followed, the company deployed a special team of employees to speed up the payment of claims.

On a lighter note, each year MetLife sponsors the MetLife Classic college basketball tournament at the University of San Francisco. Those with an eye to the sky might glimpse one of MetLife's blimps floating over other sporting events.

These types of service-oriented endeavors certainly have fueled MetLife's steady growth into one of the world's preeminent corporations.

At the beginning of 1997, MetLife had more than $1.6 trillion of insurance policies in force, and the Company's assets under management exceeded $275 billion. MetLife's size, financial stability and consistently high ratings make it a significant force in the insurance and financial-services market-

places. In August of 1996, MetLife further strengthened its position when it merged with the New England Mutual Life Insurance Company, the oldest mutual life insurance company in the country.

A recent reorganization at MetLife positively affected the Company's Bay Area operations. MetLife streamlined its business operations by consolidating a number of its smaller agencies and folding them into larger agencies that were positioned in strategic geographical locations. The changes enabled the Company to better achieve its number-one goal: excellent customer service.

One way MetLife follows through on its philosophy that excellent customer service grows business is by making sure its agents know their stuff. The

Company has put in place a comprehensive training program for new agents.

As the millennium approaches, MetLife continues to expand its portfolio of services. In addition to life insurance, MetLife offers annuities, group insurance, mutual funds (through a subsidiary, MetLife Securities, Inc.) and a brokerage service that offers such products as disability income insurance, long-term care insurance and individual health insurance.

By continuing to adhere to its sound business principles of building lasting relationships with its customers, maintaining its financial strength, and sticking to its high standards of trustworthiness and integrity, MetLife can lead the insurance industry into the 21st century. A961217A

Employees enthusiastically participate in a classic display of MetLife's community involvement.

BANK OF CANTON OF CALIFORNIA

The Bank of Canton of California's headquarters are housed in this architecturally-acclaimed building.

Gracing the wall of the Bank of Canton of California's corporate headquarters is the maxim that guides the institution: "Honest banking." More than a simple slogan, these two words describe the Bank's commitment to excellent customer service and to the fiscally conservative policies that ensure the Bank of Canton of California's continued success.

A mid-sized bank offering the resources of a large bank while maintaining the superior customer service of a smaller institution, the Bank of Canton of California operates seven branches throughout the state. Five are located in the Bay Area. The Bank also maintains an office in Taiwan, a banking facility in the Bahamas, and relationships with correspondent banks around the world.

Founded in 1937 (the same year the Golden Gate Bridge was opened), the Bank of Canton of California was established to serve the financial needs of San Francisco's Chinese community. The location of the Bank's impressive high-rise headquarters, nestled between the city's bustling Financial District and the busy streets of Chinatown, symbolizes the institution's original role as a bridge between the two communities. The clientele of the nation's oldest Chinese bank has expanded to include all segments of San Francisco's diverse population.

Under the guidance of the Bank's Board of Directors, of which H. P. Chia has served as chairman and CEO since 1985, the Bank of Canton of California continues its tradition

The Bank of Canton of California carefully preserved and restored the entire Subtreasury Building which is recognized as a California State Historical Landmark. The Pacific Heritage Museum, which displays exhibits of artistic and cultural achievements of peoples on both sides of the Pacific Basin, is now located the building.

of contribution to these communities. Among its most notable endeavors, the Bank runs the Pacific Heritage Museum, which showcases the artistic and cultural accomplishments of people living on both sides of the Pacific Basin. Also, the Bank campaigned to keep San Francisco's cable cars running; offers housing to low-income seniors; maintains a scholarship fund at the University of California, Berkeley; and launched a major clean-up effort in Chinatown and a program to "light-up and clean-up" the Tenderloin neighborhood. In recognition of the Bank's contribution and commitment to the community, former San Francisco Mayor Frank Jordan declared July 15, 1994 as "Bank of Canton Day."

In May of 1987, to mark the 50th Anniversary it shared with the Golden Gate Bridge, the Bank gifted City of San Francisco with the Bank of Canton of California Commemorative Garden. In the garden, a marble plaque reads: ". . . . this Garden honors the workers who built the bridge which, as a symbol and monument, links the peoples of the Pacific Rim and the Western World in hope, freedom, peace and brotherhood."

Such idealism and integrity are what shape the vision of this unique, community institution. The challenge for the next century is to build upon the foundation established in more than 60 years of excellence in service.

ERNST & YOUNG

One of the world's foremost accounting firms, Ernst & Young has chosen the economically and creatively fertile San Francisco Bay Area as the hub of its Pacific Northwest operations. San Francisco's diverse environment—which fosters the growth of Multimedia Gulch's online-content developers, the garment district's dynamic designers and other creative enterprises—allows Ernst & Young to work with some of the world's best and brightest.

At the same time, foundation clients such as landmark San Francisco financial institutions Transamerica and Bank of America connect Ernst & Young to the city's economic bedrock. One thing is certain: whether serving fledging startups or the biggest names in the corporate world, Ernst & Young remains committed to putting its clients' needs first.

The New York-based firm emphasizes the quality of the people it hires, ensuring that Ernst & Young's clients will continue to receive the experienced professional services to which they have become accustomed. Like many of the companies it serves, Ernst & Young has grown rapidly while continually concentrating on bringing talented creative thinkers into its fold.

Focusing on the technology, financial-services, consumer-products and healthcare industries, Ernst & Young's client list reads like a Who's Who of international commerce. A quick look reveals such major players as Coca-Cola, McDonald's and Mobil. San Francisco's position as a high-tech hotbed (and its proximity to the South Bay's Silicon Valley) enables Ernst & Young to successfully court companies like Intel, Silicon Graphics, Genentech and Netscape that are blazing trails in the booming information, communications and entertainment industries.

Ernst & Young is a good corporate citizen as well, supporting a wide variety of charitable organizations with time, energy and financial resources of its Partners, as well as its employees. Ernst & Young nurtures a full spectrum of cultural community development and outreach groups.

In the 21st century, Ernst & Young plans to leverage its experience, its commitment to quality, and its worldwide leadership position to retain its statute as the top accounting firm in the world. The company's premier San Francisco office should play a pivotal role in Ernst & Young's march toward market domination.

Ernst & Young; Photographer-Tod Gilford

John F. Nicolai, Office Managing Partner, and Roger F. Dunbar, Area Managing Partner.

SAN FRANCISCO BUSINESS TIMES

The San Francisco Business Times is the only publication entirely devoted to comprehensive news coverage of business in Alameda, Contra Costa, Marin, San Mateo, and San Francisco counties. Filling a niche left by local dailies and national business publications, the newspaper is a must-read for anyone doing business in the Bay Area. The Business Times is credited with editorial excellence, paid circulation, loyal active readers, and an outstanding environment of timely local news for more than 53,000 Bay Area readers each week.

An astounding 84 percent of the Business Times' 17,000 paid subscribers are members of top and middle management, and 50 percent are owners or partners of their own businesses. These affluent and influential readers are the business people who shape the present and future of the Bay Area's vibrant economy.

Special publications include the Health Care Quarterly, Small Business Resource Guide, Technology 2000, International Trade Resource Guide, Greater Bay Area Women in Business, Bay Area Money, Office Leasing

Guide, Top 100 Fastest-Growing Private Companies, Entrepreneur of the Year, Market Fact Guide, Where to Meet, Top 100 Fastest-Growing Private Companies, and Top 200 Public Companies.

The popular Book of Lists is widely considered the Bay Area's most valuable business reference guide. It is a compilation of the San Francisco Business Times weekly Top 25 Lists of the biggest and most profitable business enterprises. Published annually, the Book of Lists is a publication readers turn to time and again for information they are unable to find anywhere else. Though the Book of Lists is distributed through retail outlets, it is deliverable free of charge to Business Times' subscribers.

In addition to publishing timely news and information, the San Francisco Business Times hosts a number of business-information and networking forums throughout the year, including workshops for small business, and seminars on the business of health care, real estate, technology, international trade, finance and management.

The San Francisco Business Times is a member of American City Business Journals Inc., a Charlotte, North Carolina-based newspaper chain that operates 35 thriving regional business newsweeklies throughout the country.

The Business Times is credited with editorial excellence, paid circulation, loyal active readers, and an outstanding environment of timely local news for more than 53,000 Bay Area readers each week.

The popular Book of Lists is a compilation of the San Francisco Business Times weekly Top 25 Lists of the biggest and most profitable business enterprises.

SANWA BANK CALIFORNIA

Sanwa Bank California's headquarters are located in Los Angeles, California.

The growth of Sanwa Bank California over the past three years has resulted from the creation of a variety of products and services. These underscore the bank's desire to act on its longstanding promise — to provide all segments of the state's population with a full range of services. With a network of more than 100 offices statewide, assets of nearly $8 billion and some 3,000 employees, Sanwa now stands alone as California's fourth-largest bank.

So successful has the bank been in meeting the needs of the various communities it serves throughout the state, that it is one of the very few banks in the state to have received the coveted "outstanding" rating from the Federal Deposit Insurance Corporation (FDIC) for its Community Reinvestment Act (CRA) programs and services. This landmark achievement was announced by the FDIC in December.

In addition to the headquarters in Los Angeles (shown above), Sanwa also maintains regional offices in San Francisco and Fresno.

Among the Sanwa programs specifically cited by the FDIC were:

■ *Affordable housing financing,* including the Sanwa First-Time Home Buyers Program, Community involvement Program and Community Partnership Program, all of which allow for special underwriting guidelines, minimal down payments, and low or no closing costs for home purchases.

■ *High Loan-to-Value Program,* which was developed to accommodate borrowers in the declining California real estate market. Under this program, the bank offers home-equity loans and credit lines up to 100 percent of a property's appraised value.

■ *International Mortgage* Program, developed and implemented to provide home mortgage financing to new immigrants who characteristically do not have extensive credit histories, or long-term employment or residency status.

■ *Student Banking Program,* which offers students an economy checking plan with limited service charges, a secured MasterCard or VISA credit card and a pre-paid telephone charge card.

The bank's technology-oriented services — PC Homebanking, World Wide Web site on the Sanwa Telephone Banking Center — were also commended by the FDIC as strong factors in determining the outstanding rating.

During the past 12 months, Sanwa has also trained and dispersed to its network of branches nearly 100 "business bankers" specializing in working with business borrowers on solving their small-business banking

needs, including deposits, loans, credit cards and credit-card merchant accounts.

Sanwa traces its roots in the state to 1868, when its predecessor bank first opened for business in San Francisco. In 1953, Sanwa Bank Ltd. of Japan, parent bank of Sanwa Bank California, opened in San Francisco.

In 1978, after a series of acquisitions and mergers, Sanwa Bank of California changed its name to Golden State Sanwa Bank. Then, in 1986, The Sanwa Bank, Limited acquired Lloyds Bank California from Lloyds Bank PLC and merged it with Golden State Sanwa Bank to create the present day Sanwa Bank California.

The Bay Bridge.

Port of San Francisco

PCL CONSTRUCTION SERVICES, INC.

The most successful professional builders today are those that can meet aggressive project schedules, complete their projects within the owner's budget, and still adhere to the highest standards of construction quality, professionalism, and jobsite safety. PCL Construction Services, Inc., founded in 1906, is one such company. PCL delivers over $1.5 billion per year in completed projects across North America, including such high profile projects as the Honolulu Convention Center (Design/Build), the New Denver Airport Terminal and the Mall of America. In Northern California, notable recent PCL projects include:

- Packard Bell - a 1.2 million square foot North American Headquarters and computer manufacturing facility in Sacramento, CA;
- U.S. General Services Administration - the U.S. Geological Survey Laboratory in Menlo Park, CA;
- The University of California at Berkeley - "Soda Hall," a state-of-the-art computer science building on the campus at Berkeley, CA.

PACKARD BELL

PCL was ready to meet the challenge when computer manufacturer Packard Bell needed to convert 1.2 million square feet at the former Sacramento Army

Depot into a massive computer manufacturing facility in four months. In a modified design/build arrangement, PCL teamed with an architect, proposed a budget and construction schedule, and managed the reconstruction. PCL not only brought the project in earlier than scheduled, but was able to work within tight budget constraints to generate additional savings for Packard Bell.

"We excel at meeting time constraints," says PCL District Manager Dev Fraser. "Overall, time-to-market is diminishing in the industry, and we know we need to push it to the limit."

Packard Bell's new headquarters comprised of a technologically advanced manufacturing facility and support facilities for administration, food service, and employee services.

According to Packard Bell Vice President Roger Mitri, PCL's ability to set proactive production schedules and respond rapidly to changing conditions meant PCL delivered despite sometimes adverse conditions. "PCL did an outstanding job," says Mitri.

U.S. GEOLOGICAL SURVEY LABORATORY, MENLO PARK, CA

PCL's expertise in advanced technological facilities enabled it to serve the U.S.G.S. in a timely and economical fashion as well. PCL constructed a three story, 153,000 square foot structure to house research laboratories, offices and a large library. The lab facilities were completely built out with extensive fume hoods and chemical waste systems. "PCL built a state-of-the-art facility that exemplifies the meaning of quality construction and workmanship," commented

U.S. Geological Survey Laboratory in Menlo Park, California, constructed by PCL, consists of a three story, 153,000 square foot structure to house research laboratories, offices and a large library. PCL is also building the paleomagnetic laboratory at the Menlo Park site.

The new state-of-the-art computer science building at the University of California at Berkeley acts as one large "computer," complete with several miles of fiber optic cables.

Stan Lee, Contracting Officer for GSA. PCL will also build the paleomagnetic laboratory, a separate, smaller structure at the Menlo Park site.

COMPUTER SCIENCE BUILDING, U.C. BERKELEY

The 100,000 square foot, seven-level Computer Science Building at U.C. Berkeley is built like one huge computer, complete with several miles of fiber optic cabling and raised computer floors. "It is a well-built facility, and a great deal of the credit belongs to your team," stated William H. Dibbern, Director, Construction and Inspection Services for U.C. Berkeley to PCL. "The construction stayed on schedule, the job was well-organized, and the staff was responsive." Dibbern notes that this was no easy task, given the complexity of the University as a client, the stringent requirements of the project itself, and the numerous challenges posed by neighbors and city agencies.

ABOUT PCL

PCL delivers over 500 varied projects a year in North America, including advanced technology; seismic upgrades and renovations; and institutional, high-rise residential and office space. The company is growing steadily and expanding its work in complex construc-

Packard Bell needed to convert 1.2 million square feet at the former Sacramento Army Depot into a massive computer manufacturing facility in four months. PCL brought the Packard Bell Computer Manufacturing Facility in earlier than scheduled and was able to work within tight budget constraints.

tion projects that are technologically advanced. Although PCL is best known for its larger projects, the firm excels at smaller, technically complex construction projects in electronics and other advanced technology fields.

One of the top twenty-four contractors in the country as ranked by volume, PCL has 20 North American offices and over 100 construction professionals on its California construction team. The firm is 100 percent employee-owned, with more than 700 shareholders who provide the commitment and dedication to get the job done right the first time. PCL's company safety record is a leader in the industry.

A tough competitor, PCL bids on average of four projects per day in North America, and is the low- or second low-bidder on more than 50 percent of the jobs. The firm also offers formidable financial strength.

"Because of PCL's outstanding history of performance and professionalism, it has never been necessary to limit their bonding capacity - an enviable situation enjoyed by few contractors in the industry today," notes a recent letter from PCL's bonding company. PCL is a hands-on professional that understands the business thoroughly, PCL can function as any part of a construction team from General Contractor to Design-Builder.

Perhaps most importantly, PCL is an experienced, capable team player. "We're the type of company you'd want on your team," says Fraser. "We work hard to combine speed, budget considerations, and sensitivity to the end user. PCL is a value-added member of the construction team, which means the owner will have a better product because we are involved."

PCL constructed new comprehensive lab facilities for the U.S. Geological Survey Laboratory in Menlo Park, California.

DES ARCHITECTS + ENGINEERS

DES Architects + Engineers; Photographer-Vittoria Visuals (rotated, right edge of photo)

Oral-B Corporate Headquarters; Belmont, California.

When DES Architects + Engineers takes on a project, the result is a building of distinctive design and reliable substance— a good-looking building that works. DES is committed to client-architect collaboration and an approach that takes into account both aesthetic and practical needs.

Walgreen's new Bay Area distribution center is a good example. The functional task here

DES Architects + Engineers; Photographer-Jane Lidz (rotated, right edge of photo)

Walgreens Woodland Distribution Center-Executive Lobby; Woodland, California.

was to provide housing for a state-of-the-art automated distribution system that could deliver two-day turnaround on store orders. That goal was met with a design that provided an aesthetically pleasing work environment and a positive architectural statement.

Based in Redwood City, DES has designed a broad range of buildings here in the Bay Area, as well as throughout the western United States and internationally. Recently completed projects include the corporate headquarters and R&D center for Oral-B Laboratories; Stanford Hospital's intensive care units; well-known restaurateur Jeremiah Towers' Stars Restaurant in Palo Alto; Sony Computer Entertainment offices in Foster City; and Lam Research expansion in Fremont, California. International projects include Lotus International

Ltd.; Resort & Recreation Development in Guangdong Provice, Peoples Republic of China; and Y Engineering Corporation mixed use development, Manila, Philipines. Projects that have garnered awards for the firm include Apple Computer's Logistics Center, the First Nationwide Bank campus, the World Savings and Loan campus, Pacific Athletic Club's resort, Claris European headquarters, Borland International's headquarters, and Sequoia House at Sequoia Hospital.

Not surprisingly, client satisfaction is a key factor in the firm's success. "Meeting the client's requirements is our primary focus," says DES President Keith Bautista.

For the Oral-B project, DES came up with a design that created a cohesive campus despite the challenge of the site, which was bisected by a city street. "We are very pleased with our new corporate headquarters," says Barbara Kloepfer, manager of facilities and administrative services. "They are clinical without being cold and are a source of pride for both management and our employees." Kloepfer also found working with the people at DES "both exciting and rewarding. They are very bright people who are dedicated to achieving our objectives."

The management at Sequoia Hospital reports a similar experience. "We got started when we needed design direction to renovate a medical office building we had bought," says Arthur Faro, Sequoia's CEO. "We had a fixed budget, and we wanted to create medical offices that were attractive, welcoming and functional. DES met the challenge with a design that is different from our initial concept, but was developed collaboratively. They listened well and we are delighted with the finished product."

Founded in 1973, the firm has a 77-member workforce and provides a comprehensive range of services, including building master plans, programming and design, space planning, interior architecture, civil and structural engineering, and landscape architecture.

With a diverse array of services and its focus on customer needs, DES is able to foster long-term professional relationships with its clients, as it has done with Sequoia Hospital. As a result of their satisfaction with the medical office building, Sequoia went on to enlist DES for several other projects: an acute care rehabilitation center,

a remodel of the emergency department, designs for two cath labs and two operating rooms, a prenatal unit expansion, and the remodel of temporary housing for the relatives of hospital patients.

DES approaches every project with its trademark combination of quality service, creativity and cost effectiveness. The result, as one satisfied client—Larry D. McReynolds, facilities manager at Triad Systems Corporation—put it, are buildings that set "the standard by which all projects are judged."

Western Athletic Clubs-Pacific Athletic Club-Tennis, Pool and Patio; Redwood City, California.

Stars' Palo Alto Restaurant-Dining Room; Palo Alto, California.

PATSON DEVELOPMENT COMPANY

30,000-square-foot Barnes & Noble Bookstore, Walnut Creek, California.

As San Francisco rebounds from a decade-long period of slow growth in the property market, Patson Development Company, one of the last three developers to erect a high-rise office building in the financial district, is considering plans which would make it the first company to break ground on a new office building in the 1990s.

Having survived the lean years, this small-but-successful development company has revised its planning approval application for a prime site it owns at Sacramento and Front Streets. The Company had originally planned to build a two-story building on the site. If approved, the new plans, which call for adding five stories and an additional 60,000 square feet of office space, will be testament both to San Francisco's improv-

ing commercial real estate market and to the abilities of the Patson Development Company team.

Since its foundation in 1984, the Company has focused on high-quality retail, office and industrial projects throughout the Bay Area. With experience in every phase of the development process, including entitlements, design, leasing, financing, and construction and property management, the close-knit group of professionals at Patson Development Company has put together a strong track record.

Recent success stories include completed projects like the Barnes & Noble Superstore building in downtown Walnut Creek; 235 Pine Street in San Francisco, one of the last high-rise office buildings erected in San Francisco; El Camino Promenade, a 52,000-square-foot retail center in San Mateo, also housing a Barnes & Noble Superstore; a 50,000 square-foot office building in downtown Burlingame, a sensitive addition to a community known for its anti-growth development policy; and Calaveras Landing, a 190,000-square-foot "power center," anchored by Home Depot, off Interstate 880 in Union City.

In addition, Patson Development Company is in the process of completing the refurbishment of 340 Pine Street, the historic office build-

ing that houses the Company's headquarters. Patson's personality-laden penthouse office suite contains two huge chairs from the set of *The Incredible Shrinking Woman*, a pool table, darts, and a pub.

In addition to the Sacramento & Front development, projects currently in progress include the conversion of an historic, 70,000-square-foot streetcar barn, located at the corner of Geary and Arguello Boulevards in San Francisco, into a retail center leased entirely to OfficeMax. This project will be completed in May, 1997.

One of Patson Development Company's new focuses — the burgeoning demand for leisure entertainment properties — dovetails nicely with another of the Company's current projects: developing the Pavilion Building that will be attached to the San Francisco Giants' new home, Pacific Bell Park. Appointed by the Giants to make the 100,000-square-foot building

Historic Office Renovation Project 340 Pine Street, San Francisco, California.

a reality, Patson Development Company is examining the mix of theme restaurants, live-music clubs, virtual-reality uses and other retail concepts that can make the new ballpark an inviting destination all year round. As part of the complex, Pacific Bell will operate an innovative and creative Interactive Learning Center in the Pavilion Building.

This interest in leisure entertainment development is indicative of Patson Development Company's approach. The Company researches projects thoroughly before committing to them. Combine this conservative approach with the Company's strategy of pre-leasing properties before breaking ground, and its well-established connections to some of the United Kingdom's oldest and most successful property development and investment companies, and it becomes easy to understand Patson Development Company's auspicious achievements in the volatile property-development industry.

The Company's investment partners include venerable institutions such as London Merchant Securities plc, one of

the U.K.'s oldest and largest property companies and AMEC plc, the U.K.'s largest construction company. Patson also counts several substantial investment groups from around the Pacific Rim among its satisfied partners and clients. According to Ian B. Paget, one of Patson Development Company's founding partners (the other founder is David Harrison), these companies also appreciate Patson's selectivity. "They know we're picky," Paget says. "They also know we perform."

Since its beginning, Patson Development Company has been aware of its responsibility

to give back to the community. To that end, the Company donates to selected charities benefiting children, the homeless, and organizations fighting cancer and AIDS.

As Patson Development Company approaches the millennium, it plans to maintain the string of successes while expanding its operations and entering into even more high-profile projects. With San Francisco in the midst of a remarkable rebound from its trying economic times, Patson Development Company stands poised to capitalize on the City's economic rebirth.

25-story Office Tower 235 Pine Street, San Francisco, California.

45,000-square-foot Office Building 1440 Chapin Avenue, Burlingame, California.

*At dusk in San Francisco, a stroller
and his dog wander the sand strand at
St. Francis Yacht Club as the sun sinks
behind the Golden Gate Bridge.
The hills of Marin County are on
the right.*

GENENTECH, INC.

The Genentech campus of more than 20 buildings overlooks the San Francisco Bay in South San Francisco, California.

Genetech's drug Pulmozyme represented the first new therapy for cystic fibrosis patients in 30 years when it was launched in 1994.

If you were looking for a single word to sum up the activities and philosophy of the South San Francisco-based biotechnology company Genentech, Inc., that word undoubtedly would be *science*.

Genentech was founded in 1976, by venture capitalist Robert Swanson and by University of California San Francisco biochemist Herbert Boyer, just two years after Boyer and Stanford University's Stanley Cohen created the world's first recombinant DNA. With recombinant DNA technology, a gene that produces a human protein theoretically could be moved into a bacteria that reproduces itself, and thus the gene, endlessly; the result would be a little "protein factory." Swanson was enthusiastic

about the commercial possibilities of this technology and he persuaded Boyer to meet with him for ten minutes. That ten-minute meeting stretched to three hours and when it was over, Boyer and Swanson had each put up $500 and Genentech was born.

The founding of Genentech also marked the founding of the biotechnology industry. The first milestone was reached in 1977 when Genentech became the first to produce a human protein (somatostatin) in a microorganism. Within a year, Genentech scientists cloned a second protein, this time one with immediate medical potential: human insulin. Genentech eventually licensed the drug to

Eli Lilly and in 1982 it became biotechnology's first product to market.

Genentech research continues to drive the industry. Company research led to ten biotechnology-based products — almost half of all those on the market today. Genentech is the only biotech company to have taken five of its own products from the laboratory to the marketplace.

Genentech's standing in the industry was further solidified in 1990, when Roche Holding of Switzerland bought 60 percent of the company. The $2.1 billion merger gave Genentech the significant financial backing it needed to develop the drugs in its pipeline.

Today 40 percent of company's revenues, more than twice the industry average, are reinvested in research and development. Genentech scientists are the most prolific in the industry, publishing about 250 papers in scientific journals every year — more than one paper every business day. Scientists are encouraged and funded to spend about 25 percent of their time on their own research. This policy has historically led to some of the company's most important advances, including the development of the drug Pulmozyme® for treating cystic fibrosis.

The point of all this science is to develop new drugs for unmet medical needs. This

Representing the founding of Genetech, this statue was dedicated in 1992 to the Genetech founders, Herbert Boyer and Robert Swanson, and resides in the courtyard of Genentech's modern research facility.

highly rigorous process involves meeting a host of internal criteria including scientific, manufacturing, patent, and economic concerns, as well as passing the preclinical and clinical trials required by regulatory agencies. Genentech prides itself on a pipeline of products in clinical development that is widely recognized as one of the best in the industry.

Genentech currently manufactures and markets five products in the U.S.:

- *Pulmozyme®*, the first new drug to treat cystic fibrosis in more than thirty years;
- *Activase®*, a tissue-plasminogen activator used to dissolve blood clots in the arteries of heart-attack patients or in the lungs;
- *Protropin®* and *Nutropin®*, human growth hormones for treating children with growth hormone inadequacy and

growth failure due to chronic renal insufficiency (Nutropin® only) — Nutropin® also comes in a liquid version, Nutropin AQ™;

- *Actimmune®*, a drug for the treatment of chronic granulomatous disease, a rare, inherited deficiency of the immune system that primarily afflicts children.

Research interest in a drug does not stop once it is brought to market. One of the features that distinguishes Genentech from its competitors is the continuing study it conducts on patients using its drugs. This tracking gives physicians valuable data on treatment outcomes and safety.

Genentech also takes seriously its responsibility to the community. In 1986, the company instituted the Uninsured Patients Program to provide human growth hormone free

of cost to uninsured patients in the United States who otherwise could not afford it. Today all of its drugs are available under similar programs. In 1995 alone, the company provided $26 million worth of pharmaceuticals free of charge to un- or under-insured patients in the U.S.

Another area of particular interest to both the company and its individual employees is science education. In addition to donating funds to local schools through the independent Genentech Foundation for Biomedical Sciences, in 1993 Genentech launched a program to enhance the teaching of science in high schools across the country.

Called Access Excellence, the $10 million multi-year program provides an online site on the

Internet (web address: http://www.gene.com/ae) where teachers can "gather" to trade lesson plans and science information. Every high school teacher who applies to the program is given a free online computer account. The 100 teachers who are selected for the program every year are each given a computer and brought to Genentech to attend a summit where they can meet and discuss common interests.

In the years ahead, Genentech will play to its strengths, moving even more promising products from research to development each year. That is good news for people coping with serious illnesses, because what Genentech's commitment to science may ultimately mean is longer, healthier lives for people everywhere.

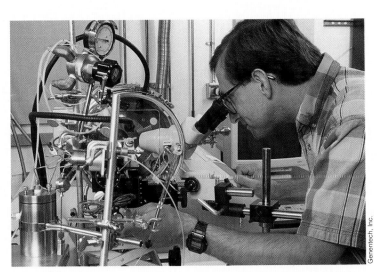

Genentech scientists rely on state-of-the-art science and technology — and old fashioned ingenuity and collaboration — to discover new weapons against disease.

LAM RESEARCH CORPORATION

Lam Research Corporation is headquartered in Fremont, California and employs over 5,000 people worldwide.

Whether or not you have heard of Lam Research Corporation, if you have a computer, cellular phone or anti-lock brakes, there is an excellent chance you have indirectly purchased its products. Lam is the world's number-one supplier of plasma etch equipment, used to perform a key step in the manufacture of semiconductor chips. While most of us tend to think of computers when we hear the word "chip", less than 50 percent of the devices Lam's tools help to produce go into com-

Lam's Deep SubMicron™ (DSM™) 9800 LP CVD system was the first to successfully demonstrate the transition to 300-mm (12 inch) wafer processing for etch applications.

puters; the remainder become parts of everyday products ranging from high-tech toys to smart home electronics. To put the phenomenal growth of the semiconductor industry into perspective, consider that cars today have more electronic components than were in the first spacecraft. That is how far and fast technology has come, and Lam has been part of that rapid rise.

The Fremont-based company specializes in deposition and etch, two key steps that are repeated numerous times in the processing of a silicon wafer. Deposition places high-quality films on the wafer, and etch selectively removes precise portions of those films, thus creating the pattern of the integrated circuit.

When it was founded in 1980, the company was one of more than thirty jockeying for position in the etch market. Today, as a leader in the field, Lam enjoys a 30 percent share of this $3 billion market.

Lam has experienced rapid expansion since its initial public offering in 1984. In 1985, the company employed 800 people and annual revenues totaled $34.5 million. Today, 5,000 employees work in forty offices throughout the U.S., Europe,

Japan, and Asia/Pacific. Lam reached the $1 billion mark in calendar 1995.

Lam continues to set the pace in the innovation and evolution of the industry. When the semiconductor industry began to switch from wet chemical etching to the more exacting method of dry plasma etching, Lam helped drive that transition, and also pioneered the move to single-wafer etch processing, which is now standard in the industry.

Ten years ago, the manufacture of a single chip might have entailed 60 individual process steps; today's devices can involve up to 800 steps. This growing complexity, driven by the need for greater speed and memory in chips, requires that increasingly fine design rules be etched onto the surface of the chip. Design rules continue to shrink from their already minute size of 0.5 micron (roughly 1/200 the diameter of a human hair.) Lam has already developed the etch technology to accommodate less than 0.25 micron design rules, and was the first company to introduce next-generation etch and CVD tools for deep submicron applications.

Lam's patented Transformer Coupled Plasma™ (TCP™) etch technology is a high-flow, high-density, low-pressure source which targets applications of 0.35-mm and below.

Recently, the company scored another first by demonstrating its etch and deposition capabilities on 12-inch (300 mm) wafers. With a surface area nearly two-and-a-half times that of today's 8-inch (200 mm) wafers, these devices continue the trend toward higher productivity at lower cost.

While it emphasizes innovative technology, Lam is also committed to improving and enhancing its existing product lines and support services. For example, the inaugural etch product, now fifteen years old, is still used in applications that require high volume and low cost. In fact, the first such system ever sold by the company was recently upgraded and reinstalled at a customer's facility.

A focus on quality and customer satisfaction is fashionable in today's marketplace. At Lam, these ideals have been a tradition since Roger Emerick became chairman and CEO in 1982 and shaped the company into a collaborative, customer-driven organization that delivers on its promises. Lam's success can be seen both in the company's bottom line and in the long list of customer satisfaction awards, including the first IBM Technology Product Division's Customer Satisfaction Award, SEMATECH's Total Quality Award, Intel's Preferred Quality Supplier Award and National Semiconductor's Top Supplier Award. Lam has made the Ten-Best, an independent survey by market researcher VLSI Research, Inc. of the best process-equipment companies worldwide, every year since the list's inception over eight years ago.

With over 3,500 employees in the Bay Area, Lam collaborates with the community, contributing to organizations that enhance the cultural life of the area. The company has also formed a number of educational partnerships with schools in Fremont, within the Silicon Valley, and around the world.

Despite its success, Lam is determined not to take its dominance in the market for granted. As Director of Corporate Communications Karen McLennan puts it, "We are a leader in the industry, but we certainly don't rest on our laurels." Clearly, the emphasis is still on the customer and that is where it is going to stay. "If we continue to put our customers first," McLennan notes, "everything else will follow."

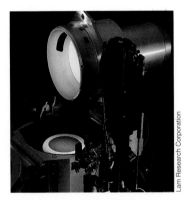

The TCP™ 9100 oxide etch system is the newest member to the production-proven Transformer Coupled Plasma™ (TCP™) family, which includes the TCP 9400 SE poly etch system and TCP 9600 SE metal etch system.

SciClone Pharmaceuticals

Image Copyright © 1996 PhotoDisc, Inc.

There is a San Mateo company that could change the world with its products — drugs that may prove to be key treatments for some of the world's most serious diseases.

The company is SciClone Pharmaceuticals Inc. and its lead drug is ZADAXIN®, thymosin alpha 1. SciClone acquires, develops and commercializes pharmaceuticals in targeted worldwide markets for chronic and life-threatening diseases, including hepatitis B and C, HIV and cystic fibrosis. The pri-

mary focus is on acquiring compounds, in various stages of clinical development, that are specialist oriented, address a significant unmet medical need and have a suggested market size that affords a major opportunity.

ZADAXIN, SciClone's flagship product, shows signs of remarkable versatility. Developed to treat hepatitis, it has shown promising results in clinical trials for other life-threatening diseases such as non-small cell lung cancer, melanoma, and AIDS.

Unlike many of its counterparts, SciClone was started in 1989 with management dollars, not venture capital, when Thomas Moore, a Honeywell software expert, and Nelson Schneider, a Wall Street analyst, licensed the drug thymosin alpha 1 for commercial development. Moore and Schneider brought in UCSF scientist John Baxter and Moore's Honeywell marketing colleague Charles Yazel. Three years later, SciClone went public, and in 1993, secured approval to market ZADAXIN commercially to treat hepatitis B in Singapore.

As a result of extensive and continuing clinical testing, ZADAXIN was recently approved as a treatment for hepatitis B in the Philippines and China and is now pending review by the Ministries of Health in Hong Kong, Mexico, India, Indonesia, Malaysia, and Cyprus. In addition, Phase III clinical trials will be, or have been, conducted in Taiwan, Italy, Japan, and the United States. In keeping with its international marketing focus, the company has established operating subsidiaries in Japan, Singapore and Taiwan, as well as an Asia-Pacific regional headquarters in Hong Kong.

A DEVASTATING DISEASE
ZADAXIN's primary indication thus far has been for the treatment of hepatitis B, a disease afflicting hundreds of millions of people around the world and killing some two million each year. A contagious disease caused by viral infection, hepatitis B can lead to chronic liver disease, cirrhosis, or even primary liver cancer.

Until now, only one drug, alpha interferon, had been approved by the FDA for treatment of chronic hepatitis B, and its usefulness is clearly limited — only 20 percent to 40 percent of patients respond to it, and it has a number of detracting side effects.

Although a vaccine has been available since 1981, it is estimated that five percent of the world's population, 300 million people, may currently be carriers of hepatitis B (HBV). Hepatitis C, which is much more likely than HBV to lead to a chronic infection, remains largely a mystery disease. The virus itself was only discovered in 1987, and there is still no vaccine for it. Although some of the ways that the virus is transmitted are known (via blood, other bodily fluids, or contaminated needles) in more than 40 percent of patients the source of infection is unknown.

PROMISING TREATMENTS
ZADAXIN may be the answer for those who sufferer from hepatitis B & C. A peptide originally isolated from the thymus gland and now produced through chemical synthesis, the drug works by stimulating the immune system and promoting the growth of T-cells. This is what makes it a promising treatment for hepatitis and several other serious diseases that damage the immune system, including HIV, melanoma, and non-small-cell lung cancer.

Additional good news about ZADAXIN is that it has been shown to be extremely safe and well-tolerated. Research has found no evidence of toxicity, and there have been no reports of drug-related side effects in the more than 2,000 patients studied to date.

On another promising front, SciClone has recently licensed CPX from the National Institutes of Health (NIH) as a potential treatment for cystic fibrosis. Cystic fibrosis (CF) is the most common severe genetic defect in the U.S. population, affecting approximately 30,000 people in the U.S. and 55,000 worldwide. CF is caused by a mutation in the cystic fibrosis transmembrane conductance regulator (CFTR) gene, which leads to poor chloride secretion and a build-up of sodium. This imbalance clogs the lungs and digestive tract, resulting in recurring respiratory infections, progressive lung damage, malnutrition and slow growth.

CPX is a "gene-assist" therapy that is believed to bind to the CFTR gene and stimulate it to

properly perform its chloride secretion function. In an in vitro study performed by the NIH on explanted human epithelial cells from the respiratory tracts of CF patients, CPX effectively stimulated the export of chloride ions. Clinical trials are scheduled to begin in the United States in early 1997.

THE BUSINESS OF
FINDING A CURE
Given the number of people across the globe who are already affected and the rate at which diseases like hepatitis are spreading, the race to find cures also represents a tremendous business opportunity for the companies who reach the finish line first. Fortune magazine reports that, in terms of dollars spent on

treatment, chronic viral hepatitis is the second largest infectious disease worldwide, after malaria, at $2.4 billion.

The results of on-going clinical trials and recent approvals in Asia have put SciClone in the forefront of those companies that are headed to market with treatments. According to analysts who follow SciClone, ZADAXIN "appears to be the heir apparent" in Asia, one of the world's largest markets for chronic hepatitis B treatment.

This is even more impressive when one considers what a relatively small company SciClone is, with fewer than 40 employees worldwide. SciClone is a small company closing in on one of the biggest health problems of our time.

Image Copyright © 1996 PhotoDisc, Inc.

OLYMPIAN

To commercial customers, Olympian sells refined petroleum products at Olympian's own automated fueling stations, in bulk to large clients, and to other oil companies.

Olympian founded the Commercial Fueling Network (CFN), a nationwide association of independent fuel marketers that also operate fueling stations for commercial sales. Operating much like ATM networks, participants issue cards that will work at their own sites as well as at the sites of other participants.

One of the first independent oil marketers in the Bay area, Olympian Oil Company was founded in 1954 in South San Francisco by Fred Bertetta Sr. In 1981, he passed the torch on to his son, Fred Jr., who serves as President. Fred Jr., along with Bonnie Addario and George Chammas (both Senior Vice Presidents), runs the company today.

The largest independent West Coast marketer of petroleum products, Olympian's operations are diverse. Olympian's retail business includes ten gas stations in the Bay Area that it operates directly and that carry Olympian's name, and forty dealer-operated stations around northern California that carry

three brand names: Olympian, Chevron, and Texaco. The stations also carry lubricants under names such as Kendall, Castrol, Chevron, Shell, and Texaco.

Since 1979, Olympian has expanded greatly by focusing more on the commercial segment of the petroleum industry. To commercial customers, it sells refined petroleum products at Olympian's own automated fueling stations, in bulk to large clients, and to other oil companies. It also sells lubricants to both end users and resellers. An engineering and environmental division, Accutite, does a wide variety of environmental work and specializes in petroleum remediation (the process of removing contaminants from soil and water). Olympian's Gulf Transportation division hauls both for their own operations and for outside parties.

In 1987, Olympian founded the Commercial Fueling Network (CFN), a nationwide association of independent fuel marketers that also operate fueling stations for commercial sales. Operating much like ATM networks, participants issue cards that will work at their own sites as well as at the sites of other participants. CFN has grown to become one of the largest networks of its kind in the United States.

CFN is in the midst of a major upgrade of its card services. Usually when you swipe a card through a machine, at most only two items are checked: the PIN number and whether or not the card is valid. If for some reason this information must be changed, it is necessary to issue a new card. What CFN is introducing is a system that, in addition to checking these two items, controls how many times the card can be used, in total or per day; what days, what times of day; how many gallons; even what type of fuel. The user sets and controls all of these features and can change them by simply sitting down at a computer. For example, a fleet manager with a fleet of utility vehicles can assure that its drivers buy only a certain number of gallons of diesel fuel between 9 a.m. and 5 p.m. and only on Mondays, Wednesdays, and Fridays. They can use the Internet to set—or instantly change—the exact profile they want on each card, offering a tremendous amount of control while tailoring the program to their needs.

Participants in CFN can see on their computer screens transactions taking place at their fuel

Olympian's Gulf Transportation division hauls both for their own operations and for outside parties.

pumps as these transactions are actually taking place. This feature offers total fuel management and puts the fleet operator in the driver's seat. Customers can also call an 800 number to get information about CFN locations, weather, road conditions, and much more — offering service beyond the pump.

Fred Bertetta Jr., President.

Olympian is proud to be known in the industry as a pioneer in making clean fuels—such as compressed natural gas (CNG), methanol, and propane—available to the public. In partnership with Pacific Gas & Electric, it started offering CNG five years ago, building northern California's first CNG facility in South San Francisco. Committed to the environment and to the future of the fuel industry, Olympian also offers methanol and propane at some of its sites and accommodates customers whose fleets run on natural gas.

The latest expansion of Olympian's service stations is a state-of-the-art auto and truck center on E. Grand Avenue in South San Francisco. Selling to both retail and commercial customers, it features a truck wash and dryer as well as a car wash, a truck scale, truck parking and shower facilities. There will be a Starbucks Coffee and a Wendy's. A Texaco Star-Mart convenience store will be open 24 hours.

In reflection of the generosity of the Bertetta family, Olympian Oil Company has been actively involved in giving to the community since its founding. Every year in the San Francisco Fire Fighters Toy Program, Olympian donates the fuel and oil to run the trucks that deliver toys to disadvantaged children at

Christmas. Olympian contributes both time and money to the San Francisco Child Abuse Council; other charities include the Children's Garden, Mills Peninsula and Seton Hospitals, and the Peninsula Association for Retarded Children and Adults (PARCA). In 1996, the Festa Italiana of San Mateo County named Fred Bertetta Jr. Man of the Year for his outstanding contributions to the community.

Today, Olympian Oil Company continues in the tradition of entrepreneurship and civic duty that has been the company's hallmark for more than 40 years.

INTEGRATED SYSTEMS, INC.

*Standing from left to right:
Greg Olson (VP, Marketing); Naren
Gupta (Chairman and Founder);
David Stepner (VP, Research &
Development); Andy Pease (VP, North
American Sales); Janice Waterman
(VP, Human Resources); David St.
Charles (President & CEO). Not shown
in photo: Tony Tolani (VP, Far East
Operations); Hamid Mirab
(VP, European Operations).*

Integrated Systems, Inc. (ISI) designs, develops, markets and supports software products for embedded microprocessor-based applications. Embedded microprocessors are used to add functionality and intelligence to a variety of products and to operate as an integral part of these products, generally without any direct human intervention.

In other words, this high-tech company, nestled in the heart of Silicon Valley, offers software that consists of a real-time operating system and a series of modules and design tools that aid the development of embedded applications. ISI's products are designed to enable users to accelerate the design, development, debugging, implementation and maintenance of embedded software, ultimately reducing expense, increasing functionality, enhancing performance and improving reliability and ease of use. The Company markets telecommunications and data communications, automotive, multimedia, and consumer and office/industrial automation.

Named in 1994 as one of San Francisco Chronicle's "Top 100 Bay Area Companies" and in 1995 as one of Software Magazine's "Top 100 Independent Software Companies," and Upside Magazine's "Upside 200 Companies," ISI is almost twice the size of its nearest competitor. "Since ISI's inception more than 15 years ago, our mission has been to innovate the most effective tools for our customers. We are pleased that today Integrated Systems' software is used in millions of products worldwide," said David St. Charles, president and chief executive officer of ISI.

Founded in 1980 by Chairman Naren Gupta, ISI's mission is to help its customers increase product-functionality, time-to-market, and cost-reduction requirements. ISI reported $84.4 million in total revenues for the fiscal year ending February 29, 1996, an increase of 45% over the previous year. Committed to providing a full range of solutions for its customer base, ISI augmented its core capabilities by acquiring TakeFive Software, Inc., Diab Data, Inc., Case Tools, Doctor Design, Inc., and Epilogue Technology during 1995 and 1996. Headquartered in Sunnyvale, California, ISI has nearly 500 employees worldwide including Asia, Europe, and North America.

Integrated Systems, Inc.

TCSI CORPORATION

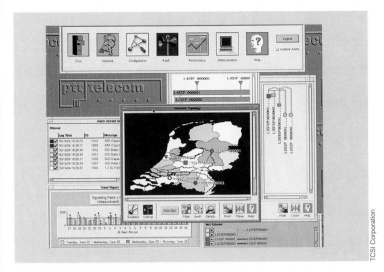

PTT Telecom Netherlands asked AT&T and TCSI to provide an integrated service management (ISM) solution for ISDN service. Deploy-ment of these advanced services enabled users to send phone, fax, and digital data on a single line using public networks. PTT's ISDN network management system is now operational 7 days a week, 24 hours a day, with only the scheduled 20 minutes of downtime for maintenance every two months.

The introduction of new technologies and recent deregulation in the telecom industry has intensified competition among the existing operators of public communications networks and encouraged the rapid entry of new service providers. To remain competitive, network operators, whether established or emerging, are continually seeking to differentiate themselves by improving upon existing service offerings and accelerating the time-to-market for new services, while simultaneously trying to keep costs down and improve efficiency.

This is where TCSI Corporation is making a difference. TCSI provides software products, services, and solutions to the telecom industry worldwide. Service providers and equipment manufacturers deploy TCSI's software to enable a range of new customer services, automated processes, and the management of broadband,

wireless, and intelligent networks. The company's software is used by some of the world's leading telecom companies, including BellSouth, GTE, Korea Mobile Telecom, Nippon Telegraph & Telephone, Lucent, Bell Atlantic, Motorola, and PTT Telecom Netherlands.

Just what does TCSI's software do? Take the example of customers who want to add call waiting or a second phone line to their existing telephone service. They must first contact their local carrier. That request then goes through dozens of data bases, including service activation, billing, marketing, network configuration, and repairs, in order to be fulfilled. This often takes several days, as each of these databases is typically operated separately and often updated manually. TCSI's software enables a telecom service provider to introduce and activate new services immediately, by replacing these decade-old legacy systems with software that can automate the processes and link the databases. The result is service in minutes or hours, rather than days.

TCSI's solutions are based upon its flagship software product, Object Services Package (OSP) and the company's extensive experience in product development and customized services for the telecom industry. The

company works closely with each of its customers to develop software solutions that incorporate TCSI's expertise, as well as that of its customers. Another important component of TCSI's solution is its mentoring services, which enable a customer to utilize their own internal resources to manage and enhance their networks in the future.

TCSI was founded in 1983 and completed an initial public offering in 1991. Based in the San Francisco Bay area, the company has offices in North America, Europe, and the Pacific Rim. With a core management team of industry professionals, experienced software designers, engineers, programmers, and science professionals, TCSI is emerging as a leader in the rapidly changing telecom industry.

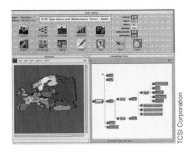

Motorola and TCSI have a worldwide master agreement providing Motorola with network management systems to control diverse cellular network equipment. Motorola licensed TCSI's Object Services Package (OSP) as a development environment for building Operations and Maintenance Centers for GSM and SuperCell systems. Teams of engineers from Motorola and TCSI are working together at different sites worldwide to specify, design, and deliver applications based upon TCSI software.

Seen from San Francisco's Lincoln Park at sunrise, the Golden Gate with its graceful garland is indeed "a miracle of nature illuminated by a flash of genius."

Part Two

MANUFACTURING AND AGRIBUSINESS

USS-POSCO Industries

The USS-POSCO Industries (UPI) steel-finishing plant in Pittsburg, California, has produced steel products continuously for 86 years. Over the last decade, UPI has become a textbook example of a company formed in one corporate tradition which was modernized and transformed to excel in another.

From its founding in 1910, in one building with a single 150-ton open-hearth furnace, the Pittsburg facility expanded to become a "one-stop shop" for virtually all steel needs: wire, nails, wire rope, pipe, reinforcing bar and flat-rolled products. After U.S. Steel acquired the plant in 1930, it supplied steel products for major public works projects including the San Francisco/Oakland Bay Bridge, and was a key supplier for the shipyards and other military projects during World War Two.

The plant struggled along with the rest of the American steel industry in the 1960's and 1970s to meet competition from the growing use of alternative materials, such as aluminum and plastic, and from foreign producers with newer equipment embodying more advanced technology. By the 1980s, U.S. Steel began looking for a partner to share the cost of modernizing the 500-acre facility.

THE MODERNIZATION PROJECT

In 1986, U.S. Steel found its partner in Pohang Iron & Steel Company (POSCO) of Korea, the fastest-growing steel producer in the world. Together, U.S. Steel and POSCO would complete a modernization project and revitalize the production facilities.

By 1989, $450 million had been invested—one of the largest expenditures ever made to upgrade a California manufacturing facility. The result was one of the most advanced and environmentally sound steel-finishing plants in the world.

Today, UPI ships more than 5,000 tons of steel every day to customers throughout the western United States, Canada, Mexico, and the Pacific Rim. It converts hot-rolled coils of steel into three main finished steel products:

- cold-rolled sheet, used for office furniture, computer cabinets, wall panels, water heaters, refrigerators, ovens, and other appliances;
- galvanized sheet, used for metal studs, siding, roofing, decking, gutters, downspouts, highway culverts, and other construction products; and
- tin products, used for packaging food items, such as fruit, vegetables, soup, tuna, and salmon pack.

With the state-of-the-art improvements to its finishing equipment, UPI has become a world-class leader in the cold-rolled sheet market in particular, successfully competing in all areas with a superior product.

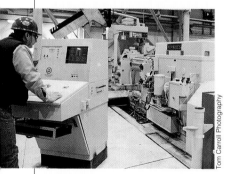

The application of high technology is evident throughout the facility, and the Learning Center at USS-POSCO provides job-related training as well as many other courses.

Cleaner air is one result of the modernization of USS-POSCO Industries, which created the most environmentally sound steel finishing facility in the world.

THE QUEST FOR EXCELLENCE: WHERE EMPLOYEE AND CUSTOMER NEEDS MEET

The goal of the modernization project was to produce both a higher-quality product and a higher level of service. UPI's objective was to become a world-class manufacturer, and the vehicle was QUEST: a model for continuous improvement that focused on Quality, Excellence, Service, and Teamwork. For the customer, that shift resulted in better products and better service; for the employees, it meant a partnership between union and management and a shift from a "piecework" perspective to a team-based approach.

THE LEARNING CENTER

Not surprisingly, the modernization of the plant meant significant changes for its employees, many of whom had been working on equipment built in the 1950s. Suddenly, people who once worked with the steel itself on the factory floor were now working with computers instead.

As one part of meeting this challenge, UPI established an on-site Learning Center, which offers job-related classes during working hours. These courses include management training, business planning, trade and craft training, statistical process control, safety programs, CPR and first aid, and computer training. The center is well used. Every day, some 50 employees attend classes there.

Learning Center courses are available not just to UPI employees, but to employees of other companies as well. Thanks to partnerships with Los Medanos College and California State University at Hayward, many additional courses applicable to an A.A., B.A., or M.B.A. degree can be taken on the UPI "campus."

PRESERVING THE ENVIRONMENT

Beyond the modernization project itself, UPI made an investment of more than $100 million to develop and install advanced environmental technologies. UPI continues to make substantial expenditures each year to minimize environmental impact, including waste minimization and pollution prevention programs.

- The plant reduced air emissions of nitrogen oxide by more than 90%, and cut water consumption by more than 60%;
- The ships that deliver hot-rolled steel to UPI make up the cleanest fleet in the world with systems that reduce diesel-engine nitrogen oxide emissions by 90%;
- UPI received a National Environmental Development Association Foundation Award in recognition of the company's strong commitment to environmental improvement and environmental quality management.

A steel worker checks quality on a production line at USS-POSCO Industries, which produces steel for products such as furniture and appliances, siding and roofing, and canned goods.

Thanks to a dramatic transformation over the past decade, UPI is one of the most advanced steel finishing plants in the world, fully competitive with other domestic and foreign producers. The combination of financial commitment, advanced technologies, management perseverance, teamwork, and a focus on quality and efficiency turned an aging and vulnerable steel plant into a modern, dynamic and environmentally sound facility.

From this control room, an operator monitors operations and data collected from more than 100 process computers. Data is then relayed to large mainframe computers.

New United Motor Manufacturing, Inc. (NUMMI)

This is the Final Inspection area on the assembly line for the Chevrolet Geo Prizm and Toyota Corolla sedan. Shown are NUMMI Quality Control inspectors inspecting each vehicle.

New United Motor Manufacturing, Inc. (NUMMI), located in Fremont, California, is the only auto manufacturer in California. In fact, it is the only auto assembly plant west of the Rockies.

NUMMI was established in 1984 as a 50-50 joint venture between Toyota Motor Corporation and General Motors Corporation (GM). For Toyota, the joint venture was the first opportunity to use its production methods in an American setting. For GM, the joint venture provided a way to learn how to build high quality cars more efficiently, using Toyota's "lean" production system. Since GM also wanted to obtain a high-quality compact car, Toyota was the perfect partner.

The NUMMI plant is over four million square feet of covered space and sits on approximately 90 acres. It employs over 4,600 team members, of whom 3,800 are hourly workers, repre-sented by the United Auto Workers, Local 2244. As a major employer in Southern Alameda County, NUMMI's payroll and benefits are approximately $300 million a year. In addition, there are more than 1,400 North American suppliers, including 500 in California, resulting in jobs for over 18,000 people. The total cumulative investment in NUMMI since 1984 is $1.7 billion. NUMMI currently builds the Chevrolet Geo Prizm, Toyota Corolla sedan and the Toyota Tacoma compact pickup truck.

Using a production system based on Toyota's provides NUMMI with the ability to meet the company's goal of

NUMMI team members volunteered their time and energy for community service projects that include painting and landscaping local schools and community centers.

building high-quality, competi-tively priced products. One of the guiding principles of its pro-duction system is "jidoka," which means that quality is ensured in the process itself rather than through inspection alone. A second guiding princi-ple is the team concept in which each team is responsible for meeting company objectives in areas such as quality, production and safety. Finally, there is the principle of "kaizen," which is the search for continuous improvement throughout the company.

NUMMI believes that no company can exist without being a good corporate citizen. So it is no surprise that the company is a leader in the com-munity, both locally and in the wider Bay Area. For example, over the years, its annual United Way Campaign has raised over $1 million, including team member donations and compa-ny matching funds. In the last six years, NUMMI has also donated cars to local Drug Abuse Resistance and Education (DARE) programs, which are administered by local law enforcement agencies. NUMMI team members also have volun-teered their time and energy for community service projects that include painting and landscaping local schools and community centers.

THE WINE ALLIANCE

Wine Alliance wineries include Atlas Peak Vineyards, Clos du Bois, Callaway Vineyard & Winery, and William Hill Winery.

Headquartered in Healdsburg, California, The Wine Alliance is dedicated to the production, sales, and marketing of truly superior wines from distinctive growing regions. It is a unique organization that shares its marketing and sales skills among four wineries which it owns and operates. Each winery fills a special niche in the super-premium/ultra-premium wine category of wines. Since its founding in 1989, The Wine Alliance has grown to become America's second largest marketer of wines of this type. Sales this year are expected to exceed one million cases.

Wine Alliance wineries include Atlas Peak Vineyards (Napa), Clos du Bois (Sonoma), Callaway Vineyard & Winery (Temecula), and William Hill Winery (Napa). The Wine Alliance also imports and markets Harveys and Domecq sherries in the United States.

The firm is owned by Allied Domecq, the international wine, spirits and retailing group. It is said that "wine is made in the vineyard" and the wineries of The Wine Alliance manage more than 1800 remarkable vineyard acres located in California's most prestigious winegrowing regions.

It is said that "wine is made in the vineyard" and the wineries of The Wine Alliance manage remarkable vineyards located in California's most prestigious winegrowing regions.

The neo-Spanish dwellings of San Francisco's Marina District overlook a public green and two yacht harbors. To the west is the graceful arch of the Golden Gate Bridge.

Part Two

HEALTH CARE AND EDUCATION

WASHINGTON HOSPITAL HEALTHCARE SYSTEM

Washington Hospital Healthcare System's 308-bed acute care hospital is supported by four community clinics, an outpatient surgery center, a radiation oncology facility, a physical rehabilitation center and a catheterization laboratory.

Washington Hospital's Sub Acute Nursing Unit opened in 1996 to serve as a medical buffer for patients who no longer require the high-level (acute) care provided by a hospital, yet are not quite ready to return home.

Along the southeastern shores of San Francisco Bay lies a cluster of communities surrounded by sweeping vistas and well-planned technical and industrial parks. A high-technology center that is also home to diverse residential communities, the area has managed to keep pace with its economic growth and change while retaining much of its small-town charm.

Washington Hospital Healthcare System is an integral part of this community. As a Health Care District, not-for-profit health care provider, Washington is owned by the community, serving residents of Fremont, Newark, Union City, and part of South Hayward. Formed in 1948 by a group of public-minded citizens who wanted to bring modern health care to the communities, the Health Care District today is southern Alameda County's top health care provider.

The medical staff boasts a membership of more than 300 men and women who have trained at some of the top teaching facilities around the world. The comprehensive range of facilities and services include the 308-bed, acute-care general hospital; 24-hour emergency care; four outpatient clinics; state-of-the-art operating rooms and diagnostic equipment; a comprehensive Heart Program; the Washington Stanford Radiation Oncology Center; the Washington Outpatient Surgery Center; the Washington Outpatient Rehabilitation Center; the Washington Outpatient Catheterization Laboratory; the Washington/Packard Children's Special Care Nursery; a student health clinic serving 8,000 students at Ohlone Community College; and a new Sub Acute Nursing Unit.

Washington West—the Healthcare System's complex for community resources, medical offices, and other Washington services—opened in early 1997. One of those services is Washington's Health Insurance Information Service. Another is Washington's Community Health Resource Library. Open to the public, it features an extensive collection of the latest medical and research information available.

The Health Insurance Information Service was developed in response to the community's need for reliable health insurance information. Washington Township Health Care District created a service that provides residents with the tools to make an informed decision when selecting a health insurance plan. "People are facing a health care environment in which they must play a new and more demanding role when selecting their health insurance," says Chief Executive Officer Nancy Farber. "Our new service shows individuals that when they select a health insurance plan, it's a decision that will later determine what amount of health care will be paid for."

After years of planning and collaboration with Lucile Salter Packard Children's Hospital at Stanford, local families with sick newborns now have access to advanced medical care in their own community. The Washington/Packard Children's Special Care Nursery is the first and only level II nursery in the Tri-City area. Prior to the unit's opening in 1995, babies who required a higher level of care had to be transferred to other Bay Area hospitals capable of providing specialized newborn care. The collaboration between the two hospitals greatly benefits the community. "In the last decade, hospitals throughout our state have competed vigorously against one another for survival, which has not always benefited the communities they serve," says CEO Farber. "This special relationship between Washington Township Health Care District and Packard Children's Hospital allows the two health care organizations to work together in bringing the best in newborn care to our district."

Washington Hospital's new Sub Acute Unit serves as a transition for patients who no longer require the high-level (acute) care provided by a hospital, yet are not ready to return home. "This new service is a tremendous addition to our continuum of care for many of our patients, especially our senior citizens," says CEO Nancy Farber. "Patients in the unit will now be able to continue their recovery under the supervision of many of the same medical professionals who have served them in the acute stages of care as well." A typical patient of the Sub Acute Unit, for example, is a senior who is still recovering from hip surgery or respiratory problems and needs a few extra days of nursing or rehabilitative care before leaving the hospital.

Washington's series of programs emphasizing healthier lifestyles, earlier detection of diseases, and prevention of medical problems has grown in popularity. Each class now attracts 100 or more people on a regular basis. Sponsored in part by the Washington Hospital Healthcare Foundation, the Community Education Programs feature local physicians and other medical professionals who generously share their wealth of medical knowledge in easy-to-understand presentations.

The Health Care District's strength has been its ability to adapt and keep pace with change by introducing new programs and services. In a changing health care environment, Washington Hospital Healthcare System stands firm on its commitment to provide quality health care. Owned by the community, for the community, its determination of care is based on the community's needs. Says Chief Executive Officer Nancy Farber, "The physicians, employees, and volunteers of Washington Township Health Care District are steadfast in their resolve to provide quality care, conveniently and at an affordable cost. In a time when change is all around us, it is good that certain things remain constant."

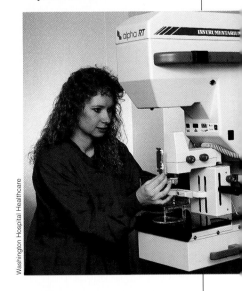

Washington's new mammography machine is more comfortable for patients and provides more detailed breast X-rays. It is just part of a $1.5 million medical imaging upgrade project to be completed in 1997.

Washington Hospital Healthcare

Washington Hospital Healthcare

Staff from the Washington/Packard Children's Special Care Nursery pose near the unit's entrance. The unit, which opened in the summer of 1995, is the first and only level II nursery in the Tri-City area.

EDEN MEDICAL CENTER

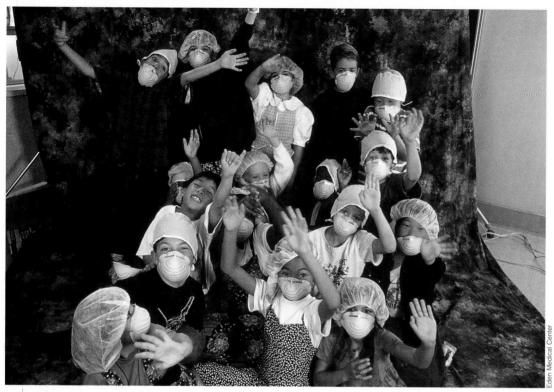

Children from local elementary schools learn about hospitals and medicine with an emphasis on fun, at Eden Medical Center in Castro Valley.

Eden Medical Center is a major regional health care center meeting the demands of today's rapidly changing health care environment. Established in 1954 to serve residents of Alameda and Contra Costa counties, the Eden Township Hospital District today operates the 324-bed, not-for-profit Eden Medical Center. Located in Castro Valley, the Medical Center includes Eden Hospital, Laurel Grove Hospital and Baywood Court Skilled Nursing Facility. The Eden Township Hospital District, led by a five-member, publicly-elected Board of Directors, offers a continuum of care encompassing emergency treatment, acute care, outpatient services, rehabilitation, and home care.

Eden's vision of a community hospital is more than just state-of-the-art skills and technology. Eden is dedicated to compassionate care that addresses the needs, and respects the dignity, of individual patients across a broad spectrum of medical practice.

Due to its designation as the regional trauma center for Southern Alameda County, Eden's Trauma Center is staffed 24 hours a day by board-certified emergency physicians, nurses, and technicians. This high level of care ensures that critically injured patients receive exceptional care in the crucial moments following a life-threatening injury.

Eden's Community Cancer Center provides information, referral, treatment, and support to cancer patients and their families. Laurel Grove Rehabilitation Hospital and the Transitional Care Center offer a complete array of inpatient and outpatient rehabilitation services to restore health and independence. In addition to rehabilitation services for those who have suffered illness or injury requiring intensive therapy in a hospital setting, the Medical Center offers physical therapy, occupational therapy, industrial rehabilitation, speech therapy, and a specialized hand therapy clinic, as well as support groups and the services of a rehabilitation psychologist.

Accredited with commendation by the Joint Commission on the Accreditation of Healthcare Organizations, the Eden Medical Center staff includes more than 350 physi-

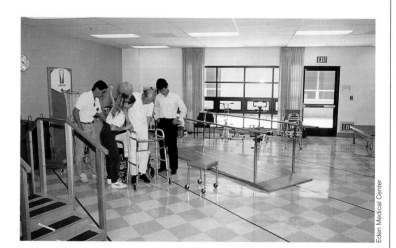

The Acute Rehabilitation Unit at Eden Medical Center in Castro Valley helps patients work to regain strength and independence following a severe illness or injury.

cians representing nearly 40 medical specialties. The Medical Center employs more than 750 full- and part-time workers, including 200 registered nurses with training in critical care, rehabilitation, emergency and trauma, psychiatry, labor and delivery, nursery care, cancer care and other areas vital to health care.

Eden Medical Center is a leader in reducing costs to better serve the 300,000 people living in the Eden Township Hospital District. The Medical Center offers more than 140 wellness programs; free breast cancer and prostate cancer screening, education, and support groups; information, referral and health programs through the Women's Center; and continuous staff training. Eden Medical Center is devoted to providing the highest quality maternity care and other medical services for women, including a modern birthing center, classes for families-to-be, childbirth preparation, and baby care.

Through programs such as PrimeTime, Eden offers a variety of support and education services to older adults, such as: diagnostic and therapeutic heart and lung services; low-cost transportation; an in-home emergency response system; senior meals; and a specialized program to return older adults

to emotional health. Eden's community education programs include heart-healthy cooking, stop-smoking classes, straight talk about cholesterol, and many other free and low-cost classes.

More than 40 years ago, the residents of San Leandro, Castro Valley, Hayward, and San Lorenzo built a hospital to meet their health needs and improve their quality of life. They established a tradition of exceptional care that comes not only from skill and technology, but from the heart—a tradition that continues to guide Eden Medical Center today. It is the people of Eden who make the difference: medical staff, employees, volunteers and supporters, who together create an exceptional environment that preserves and improves the health of the communities served by these dedicated individuals.

Eden Medical Center in Castro Valley is the designated Trauma Center for southern Alameda County and is Accredited With Commendation by the Joint Commission on the Accreditation of Healthcare Organizations.

Eden Medical Center in Castro Valley operates a Level II Intensive Care Nursery with nurses specially trained in critical care. Since the hospital opened in 1954, more than 60,000 babies have been born in Eden's maternity unit.

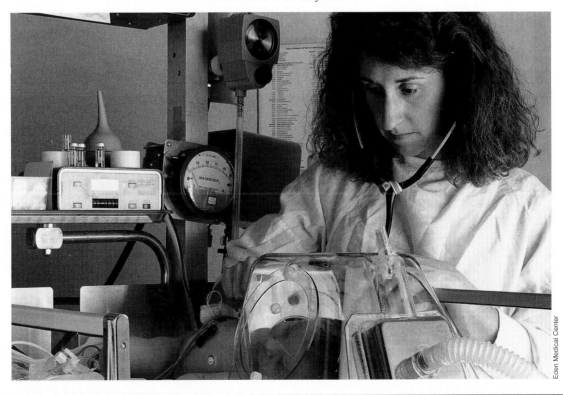

SHAKLEE CORPORATION

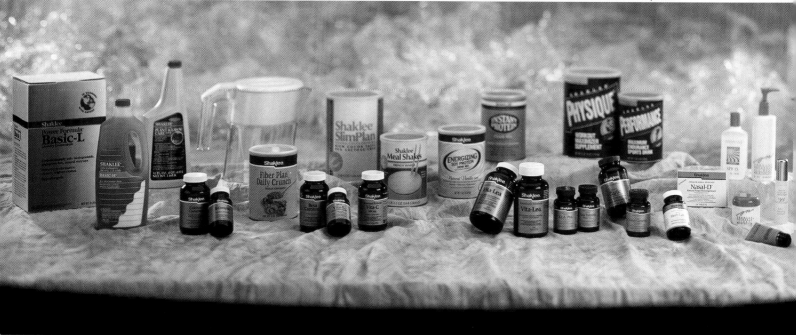

Shaklee Corporation

Shaklee Corporation manufactures Products in Harmony with Nature and Good Health®.

Shaklee Corporation

Shaklee Corporation Worldwide Headquarters, located in downtown San Francisco.

Founded by Dr. Forrest C. Shaklee, Shaklee Corporation began over 40 years ago as a small family business in the Bay Area. Dr. Shaklee was dedicated to the idea of maintaining wellness, and also believed in manufacturing products that would be good for the health of both people and the environment. Dr. Shaklee said, "I wanted a company that would improve the lives of everyone it touched."

As one of the companies that pioneered multilevel marketing, San Francisco-based Shaklee offers a person-to-person entrepreneurial marketing plan that provides unlimited earning potential. Products are sold directly to consumers by a network of thousands of knowledgeable, independent distribu-

tors and are not available in stores. Shaklee's independent business opportunities provide both economic rewards, and lifestyle and career flexibility.

Shaklee Corporation grew rapidly to become a Fortune 500 company listed on the New York Stock Exchange. Today, Shaklee Worldwide is a values-based, innovative global marketing company with operations in the United States, Canada, Mexico, Taiwan, the Philippines, Malaysia, Argentina, and Singapore; with a sister company in Japan. In 1989, Shaklee was acquired by Yamanouchi Pharmaceutical Co., Ltd., one of Japan's largest pharmaceutical companies. The combination of

the two firms has created a global entity on the cutting edge of science and technology, offering products that continue the tradition of health, wellness and high environmental standards.

Shaklee Corporation invests heavily in its research & development and manufacturing facilities and promotes the highest scientific standards in the development of new products. Shaklee Technica is the division of Shaklee Corporation responsible for scientific research & development and manufacturing. The Forrest C. Shaklee Research Center in Hayward, California, guarantees the science behind Shaklee products. It has an outstanding reputation for scientific innovation and quality. Products are made to be environment-friendly and are not tested on animals. Norman,

Oklahoma, is home to the manufacturing plant, where the most stringent pharmaceutical manufacturing standards are met. The finest natural ingredients available are used and procedures and quality assurance are state-of-the-art. Shaklee and Yamanouchi in partnership are building two new major facilities. A $23.5 million pharmaceutical manufacturing plant in Norman, and the $45 million Yamanouchi-Shaklee Pharmaceutical Research Center at Stanford Research Park in Palo Alto, California, will both be managed by Shaklee Technica.

Bear Creek Corporation, a wholly-owned subsidiary of Shaklee Corporation headquartered in Medford, Oregon, pioneered food and gifts by mail through Harry and David,

famous for its Fruit-of-the-Month Club. Harry and David, the largest direct mail marketer of gourmet fruits and foods in the U.S., has also opened 45 retail stores and plans to open more. Bear Creek also includes Bear Creek Gardens, Wholesale Division, the largest rose grower in the world, and Jackson & Perkins mail order catalogs.

In keeping with its commitment to the community, Shaklee Corporation has a long tradition of being a responsible corporate citizen. Shaklee Cares is a publicly-supported non-profit organization that aids disaster victims. In observance of the 100th anniversary of the founder's birth, Shaklee Corporation established the Community Caretaker Awards. This program recognizes people who are active leaders in their communities

Groundbreaking for Yamanouchi-Shaklee Research Center, at Stanford Research Park in Palo Alto, California.

with a grant to the community organization that each honoree names. There is also the Dr. Shaklee Memorial Scholarship program and support for environmental education programs such as Will Steger's International Arctic Project.

Dr. Shaklee dedicated himself to improving our world and the lives of ordinary people. Today, this is still the philosophy of the company he began.

Shaklee-sponsored International Arctic Project Team at the North Pole.

UNIVERSITY OF CALIFORNIA SAN FRANCISCO

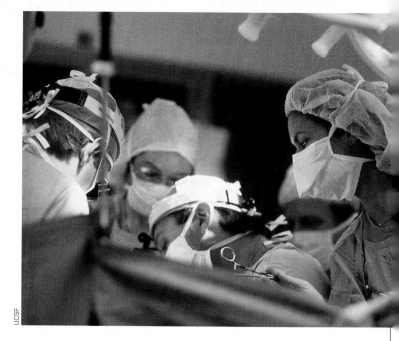

UCSF's Medical Center is consistently listed among the best hospitals in the country. Pictured below is a liver transplant operation performed at the Medical Center.

Founded in 1864 as Toland Medical College and affiliated with the University of California in 1873, the University of California San Francisco (UCSF) is the only one of the system's nine campuses devoted exclusively to the health sciences.

Its schools are among the best in the United States. The School of Medicine graduates about 140 new doctors each year. US News and World Report's latest survey of America's best medical schools ranked UCSF sixth overall among research-oriented schools, and number one in the Western United States. Fifty-three percent of the medical students enrolled are ethnic minorities; more than half are women.

The School of Nursing, founded in 1939, today graduates more than 200 nurses with advanced degrees per year. Among these are 100 master's-qualified nurse practitioners, more than at any other nursing school in the country, who are trained to deliver primary care. The school was ranked number one by US News and World Report.

The School of Pharmacy, founded in 1872 and the first in the West, turns out 120 new doctors of pharmacy a year. It was also rated the best in the country by US News and World Report.

Founded in 1881, the School of Dentistry was the first dental school west of the Mississippi. Ranked among the top public dental schools in the country, it graduates eighty dentists, sixteen hygienists, and fifteen specialists each year.

The Graduate Division, founded in 1961, attracts some of the brightest minds from all over the world to train in basic health sciences as well as related social and behavioral sciences.

Ten thousand applicants compete for 700 positions in the entering classes of these schools each year.

UCSF's Medical Center is consistently listed among the best hospitals in the country and is known worldwide for highly specialized diagnosis and treatment. Integrating research and clinical care, it is both a major teaching hospital and a community hospital. Physicians at UCSF are the ones who, literally, write the textbooks. Over 130 UCSF doctors are listed in Best Doctors in America, which ranks UCSF among the top four medical centers in the country based on the number of entries. In addition, UCSF faculty, residents, and interns provide all the patient care, teaching, and research at city-owned San Francisco General Hospital and at the San Francisco Veterans Affairs Medical Center.

UCSF is San Francisco's second largest employer, behind only the city itself. Each year it pours $1.3 billion into the Bay Area's economy. UCSF inventions and technology have created over 35 Northern California companies. One of the most influential of these discoveries was the development, with Stanford, of recombinant DNA techniques, giving rise to the entire biotechnology industry.

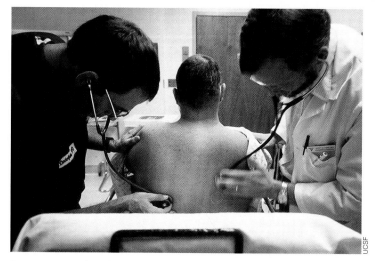

Integrating research and clinical care, UCSF's Medical Center is both a major teaching hospital and a community hospital. In addition, UCSF faculty, residents, and interns provide all the patient care, teaching, and research at city-owned San Francisco General Hospital and at the San Francisco Veterans Affairs Medical Center. Pictured above is an emergency room examination.

CITY COLLEGE OF SAN FRANCISCO

Celebrating its 60th anniversary, City College of San Francisco has earned its reputation for teaching excellence. It is one of the largest community colleges in the United States and offers the greatest educational value in San Francisco. Businesses take full advantage of this comprehensive program that links employers with the college and other workforce education partners.

With a new main library, nine campuses in San Francisco, and courses offered at more than 100 neighborhood locations, City College serves more than 65,000 students each semester and provides post-secondary education to one of every seven residents of San Francisco. City College offers courses for students who are retraining for new careers; expanding or starting small businesses; upgrading current skills; or completing two

years of undergraduate work in preparation for transfer to a four-year college or university.

"Most people have eight to ten jobs during their lives," says Dean Steven M. Glick, School of Business and Downtown Campus. "Therefore, they continually seek additional education related to their careers."

Through its Contract Education Program, City College builds training partnerships with businesses, government agencies, and community-based organizations. It helps to educate companies' workforces to become more productive, competitive, and profitable. Classes are customized to meet an organization's training needs.

"Ours is a real climb-the-ladder program," says Dr. Natalie Berg, Dean, John Adams Campus/School of Health and Physical Education. "For instance, if you've been trained

as a home health aide, with retraining you can move up to licensed vocational nurse, registered nurse, or to positions that require a bachelor's degree."

Robert F. Manlove, Ph.D., Dean, School of Science and Math, observes that the concentration of research and development in San Francisco stimulates a need for qualified technicians. City College has a Biotechnology Certificate Program that offers qualified students training as laboratory technicians in this rapidly expanding industry. Another burgeoning field is computer technology, where enrollment has increased by 23 percent this past year.

City College of San Francisco is the low-cost, post-secondary education provider in San Francisco, distinctive for the breadth of its course offerings and the excellence of its faculty. "Because we serve a diverse, multicultural population, we are the true college of the community," says Chui L. Tsang, Ph.D., Dean, School of Applied Science and Technology. "We are a teaching institution, not a research institution," emphasizes Chancellor Del M. Anderson. "Our education is personal, practical, and hands-on."

City College of San Francisco has nine campuses and more than 100 instructional sites within the City and County of San Francisco. One out of seven residents takes advantage of the educational opportunities offered by this large, urban community college.

Mark Ludak, photographer

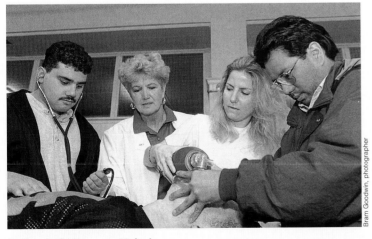

Bram Goodwin, photographer

Students in the Emergency Medical Technician (EMT) program at City College of San Francisco are taught life-saving techniques using the most up-to-date equipment available.

STANFORD UNIVERSITY

Stanford University was founded in 1885, in memory of Jane and Leland Stanford's only son, who died of typhoid at age 15.

Stanford University, one of the world's leading teaching and research institutions, is a diverse and lively forum for those addressing 21st century issues and ideas. Its 14,000 students and 1,400 faculty have helped make the San Francisco Bay Area, including the phenomenon the world knows as the Silicon Valley, the world's most innovative region, generating the ideas and products that fuel the global economy.

With one of the most distinguished faculties in the nation, Stanford has attracted world renowned scholars. They include 11 Nobel laureates, 4 Pulitzer Prize winners, and 20 National Medal of Science honorees. Stanford students are equally accomplished: 75 have been named Rhodes Scholars and 50 have been honored as Marshall Scholars. A rigorous undergraduate education leads almost ninety percent of undergraduates to enter graduate and professional schools, and encourages many to participate in a wide array of community activities through the Haas Center for Public Service.

Leland and Jane Stanford founded the University in 1885 as an enduring memorial to their only child, a son who died of Typhoid at age 15. Addressing the Stanford Board of Trustees in 1904, Jane Stanford defined the challenge for a great university: "Let us not be afraid to outgrow old thoughts and ways, and dare to think on new lines as to the future of the work under our care." Her thoughts resonate in the words of the current Stanford President, Gerhard Casper: "The true university must reinvent itself every day. ...At Stanford, these are days of such reconsideration and fresh support for our fundamental tasks — teaching, learning, and research."

Seventy-five of Stanford's 14,000 students have been named Rhodes Scholars and fifty have been named Marshall Scholars.

SAN FRANCISCO VA MEDICAL CENTER

Located on a hilltop overlooking the Golden Gate and Pacific Ocean, the San Francisco Veterans Affairs Medical Center commands one of the most beautiful views in North America. Here, a 344-bed general medical and surgical hospital, and a 120-bed skilled nursing facility, provide state-of-the-art care to veterans.

The mission of the San Francisco Veterans Affairs Medical Center (SFVAMC) includes clinical services, teaching, and advanced medical research. The Center provides acute medical and surgical care to veterans from San Francisco to the Oregon border, and tertiary care to veterans throughout the West. Clinicians at SFVAMC hold faculty appointments at the world renowned University of California at San Francisco (UCSF) School of Medicine, and SFVAMC hosts UCSF residents in virtually all specialties and subspecialties.

"The partnership between SFVAMC and UCSF provides veterans with the highest quality care," says C. Diana Nicoll, M.D., Ph.D., SFVAMC Chief of Staff.

SFVAMC has a highly regarded post traumatic stress disorder (PTSD) program. PTSD can develop after a person experiences or witnesses highly stressful or threatening events. The Medical Center also offers veterans medication and referral to other rehabilitation or social service programs. The Women Veterans Health Care program offers comprehensive health care for women veterans, including care for women suffering from PTSD.

SFVAMC is in the vanguard of the fight against HIV/AIDS, providing both cutting-edge treatment and clinical research. The Infectious Diseases Clinic provides comprehensive care to HIV patients through a multidisciplinary approach that includes an infusion center that administers chemotherapy and transfusions. The treatment of asymptomatic, HIV positive individuals includes provision of drug therapy, such as AZT.

San Francisco VA Medical Center is a major clinical research facility annually administering nearly $30 million in research grants — more than any other VA facility, and more than many university medical centers. The Medical Center's research on AIDS-related dementia may help to explain the mechanisms of other brain disorders, such as Alzheimer's and alcoholic brain disease. Heart research seeks to identify the characteristics of patients most at risk of post-operative heart attacks.

Dr. Nicoll says, "Our number one priority is patient care, but our physician education and medical research programs enable us to be a leader in those fields as well. Through these efforts we make important contributions, not only to San Francisco Bay Area veterans, but to the quality of life for all Americans."

Sunrise warms the San Francisco Bay as the Golden Gate Bridge snuggles under a blanket of fog. The Bay Bridge, just visible to the left, is spotlighted by a ray of morning sunlight.

SAN FRANCISCO HILTON AND TOWERS

The San Francisco Hilton and Towers offers 110,000 sq ft of meeting rooms, including the luxurious Grand Ballroom.

The largest hotel on the West Coast when it opened in 1964, the San Francisco Hilton was dubbed "the greatest addition to San Francisco since cable cars," by then Governor Pat Brown. With its original 1,200 guest rooms and a 19,000 square foot, column-free ballroom, the Hilton quickly became a favored venue for large events, such as the Republican National Convention, which it hosted in 1965. The Hilton also has the distinction of having hosted the Beatles during their final concert together which was held at Candlestick Park.

Occupying an entire block in the heart of the City's prestige retail, theater and entertainment district, the Hilton remains the West Coast's largest hotel. The Hilton Towers, a luxury "hotel within a hotel" added in the $210 million 1988 renovation and expansion of the Hilton complex, increased the number of guest rooms and suites to nearly 2,000. The hotel continues to invest millions of dollars in its San Francisco facilities each year to assure that Hilton remains a premier destination in a city renowned for luxurious accommodations. Generous size is important for a convention hotel, and attention to detail is essential to the quality of the guest experience. Hilton takes great care with moldings and

millwork, upholstery and window treatment. Its sunken lobby sets the tone with inlaid marble, imported carpets, and dazzling chandeliers.

Service is at the core of the Hilton experience. Five acclaimed restaurants offer a wide variety of delicious cuisine. A full-service health club and heated outdoor swimming pool cater to the fitness-conscious traveler. Well-appointed guest rooms include such amenities as in-room movies, mini-bars and hair dryers. Guests can bank 24 hours a day at an ATM inside the main lobby, or seek advice and assistance from a 24-hour guest-services hotline. The hotel's multilingual staff are ready to help the many guests not fluent in English, and hotel literature is conveniently available in several languages. The Hilton's central location puts it within easy walking distance of Moscone Convention Center, Union Square shopping, Yerba Buena Gardens cultural facilities, the theater district, and all types of public transportation.

Amid all these pleasures and comforts, Hilton also means business. The hotel offers 110,000 square feet of meeting rooms, and a state-of-the-art executive business center. In addition to the usual copy, fax and teleconferencing capabilities, the center provides color photocopying, desktop publishing, and camera-ready art work.

With its dedication to first-rate accommodations and first-class service, it is no surprise that the San Francisco Hilton has received the American Automobile Associations' Four Diamond Award in each of the last twenty years, but the Hilton is a leader in other areas as well. It is one of only two high-rise San Francisco hotels that meets the City's newest fire-protection standards, and it is one of the few hotels to reach full compliance with the Americans with Disabilities Act. The hotel has won numerous awards for its model recycling program. Since 1988, it has recycled an average of 50,000 pounds of materials a month, and the amount should increase dramatically with its recent initiation of a program to recycle directly from every guest room in the three-building complex. The hotel also has taken steps to manage energy use effectively, and has earned more than $60,000 in energy rebates and an Excellence in Energy Award from the local utility, Pacific Gas and Electric Company.

The San Francisco Hilton has earned high marks for community involvement where outreach and support are an integral part of its overall business plan. Since 1993 it has actively collaborated with local neighborhood organizations to preserve affordable housing, improve public safety, and promote economic development. An early success is an after-school program that serves the neighborhood's 4,000 children. Hilton General Manager Holger Gantz raised the initial $75,000 to establish the program, and has since formed a fundraising collaboration to maintain the project.

The San Francisco Hilton and Towers is a world-class hotel and an outstanding corporate citizen, firmly committed to serving both its guests and its community.

The sunken lobby of the Hilton sets a luxurious tone with inlaid marble, imported carpets, and dazzling chandeliers.

Occupying an entire block in the heart of the City's prestige retail, theater and entertainment district, the Hilton Hotel and Towers remains San Francisco's largest hotel.

SAN FRANCISCO GIANTS

Barry Bonds, a three-time National League Most Valuable Player and future Hall-of-Famer, is the latest in a long line of baseball superstars to play for the hometown San Francisco Giants.

San Francisco Giants; Photographer, Martha Jane

A franchise with one of baseball's most storied histories, the Giants celebrate their 40th year in San Francisco in 1997. Founded in 1883 as the New York Gothams, then renamed the New York Giants four years later, the Giants moved west to San Francisco in 1958.

Showcasing such legendary names as John McGraw, Christy Mathewson, Carl Hubbell, Bill Terry, Willie Mays, Willie McCovey and Juan Marichal throughout their history, the Giants boast the winningest record (9,156 wins, 7,810 losses) ever among National League teams—second only to the New York Yankees in all of baseball. In fact, the New York-San Francisco franchise has produced more members (47) of the Baseball Hall of Fame than any other team in the Major Leagues.

A new era of Giants baseball began in 1993, when a group of influential San Francisco businessmen headed by Peter A. Magowan purchased the 114-

year-old Major League franchise. In the initial season of new ownership, the Giants set all-time club records for victories (103) and home attendance (2.6 million) in 1993.

Yet, the club's ownership group enjoyed their greatest achievement on March 26, 1996, when San Francisco voters approved the team's new China Basin ballpark initiative by a landslide 2-to-1 margin. The Major League's first privately-financed ballpark in more than 30 years, the $255 million, 42,000-seat Pacific Bell Park is scheduled to open in April 2000, providing Bay Area baseball fans with a state-of-the-art facility for many generations to come.

The downtown San Francisco park will be located in a 13-acre, two-block area bordered by King, Second and Third streets, and on the south by China Basin. It features the most public transportation options of any ballpark in the nation. The site will be served by two rail systems, easy connections to BART (Bay Area Rapid Transit), multiple bus routes and direct north- and east-bay ferry service. Fans who drive to the ballpark will find approximately 6,500 parking spaces available within a 15-minute walk of the park, and an additional 5,000 dedicated parking spaces in the immediate vicinity of the ballpark will be reserved for Charter Seat and Luxury Suite holders. The views of the water, the Bay Bridge and the San Francisco skyline are breathtaking, and will produce the most dynamic location in America to watch Major League Baseball.

Pacific Bell Park will be a major boost to the San Francisco economy, generating $125 million and over 3,000 jobs in annual impact; and more than 3,600 jobs will be created during the building phase, which will begin in the fall of 1997.

San Francisco Giants

Pacific Bell Park, America's first privately-financed Major League ballpark in more than 30 years, will serve as the Giants' spectacular new home beginning in the year 2000.

SAN FRANCISCO CONVENTION AND VISITORS BUREAU

The debris from the 1906 earthquake and fire had barely been cleared away when enterprising San Franciscans began to think about ways to lure outsiders to their rebuilt city. As a start, they incorporated a non-profit membership organization called the San Francisco Convention & Tourist League on November 30, 1909. The League's aim, as set forth in its articles, was "to cause the cooperation of the various commercial and other business interests...to procure conventions, assemblies, and other meetings to be held at San Francisco, California." The organization changed its name to the San Francisco Convention & Tourist Bureau in 1921, and in 1952 "Tourist" was replaced by "Visitors."

During its first 53 years of operation, the San Francisco Bureau concentrated primarily on selling its product to convention groups. Opportunity to broaden its scope came in 1962 when the City allocated a portion of the revenues produced by the newly adopted hotel-motel tax to the Bureau, and designated it San Francisco's official visitor promotion agency.

Today the San Francisco Convention & Visitors Bureau is one of the largest independent visitor service organizations in the country, responsible for the care and feeding of the City's most productive economic engine. Tourism today generates more than $5 billion annually for the San Francisco economy.

It is not hard to see why. Surrounded on three sides by water, framed by two magnificent bridges, peopled by genial residents of every ethnicity, sprinkled with interesting architecture throughout 42 breathtaking hills, plied by historic and picturesque cable cars, and endowed with the history of a naughty and colorful past, San

Surrounded by water on three sides and framed by two magnificent bridges, the Bay Bridge (shown here) and the Golden Gate, the City of San Francisco is charmingly situated.

Francisco's attributes might well be taken for granted. But even the most glamorous movie queen needs a good press agent.

Now one of the nation's most venerable organizations of its kind, the San Francisco Convention & Visitors Bureau never loses sight of its mission: to market San Francisco as the premier destination for meetings, conventions, leisure and business travel. With a winning combination of strong local business partners, talented staff, incomparable natural assets and civic-minded leaders, the San Francisco Bureau is poised to round out its first century as the market leader in the field of convention and tourism promotion.

A cargo ship passes below the Golden Gate Bridge, which spans the bay's entrance from San Francisco to Sausalito.

OAKLAND RAIDERS

The Raiders' historic return to Oakland in 1995 was enthusiastically received by loyal rooters. Over one-half million fans filled the stands to personally welcome the Raiders back to the team's birthplace. Millions more faithful showed their approval by tuning into Raiders games on television.

The Raiders delivered to the Bay area its first World Championship of Professional Football in 1976 with a win in Super Bowl XI. Again in 1980, Oakland became pro football's ultimate champion with a victory in Super Bowl XV. While based in Southern California from 1982 to 1994, the Raiders gave Los Angeles its only World Championship of Professional Football with a win in Super Bowl XVIII in 1983.

After beginning in 1960 as an original member of the old American Football League, the franchise struggled to win nine of 42 games in three initial sea-

Steady guard Steve Wisniewski is a six-time Pro Bowler.

sons. In 1963, Al Davis took over as head coach and general manager of the faltering Oakland franchise and pledged to build the finest organization in sports.

The Raiders stand alone as they have appeared in Super Bowls in the 60s, '70s, and '80s and are the only original AFL team to have won a Super Bowl since 1969. The Raiders are the only AFC team to have won a Super Bowl since 1980 — and have done so twice.

Since 1967 when the Raiders won the AFL Championship and went to the Super Bowl in their first season in the playoffs, the team has been in the play-offs 18 times, played in 12 Championship games, won or shared 14 Division titles, won three American Football Conference Championships and three World Championships of Professional Football.

Seven of the great players who proudly wore Silver and Black, and owner Al Davis, already have been enshrined in the Professional Football Hall of Fame. Five Raider head coaches, including Al Davis, have been selected as Pro Football Coach-of-the-Year.

Since 1970, the Raiders have compiled a 61-31-1 record versus the NFC, going 3-1 in 1995. On Monday Night Football, the Raiders have a dominating 31-13-1 record and are 12-0 at home.

For their four decades, the Raiders defied great odds to maintain their unparalleled level of excellence. The past has been glorious, but *The Greatness of the Raiders Remains in its Future.*

Wide receiver Tim Brown led the Raiders in receptions (89), receiving yards (1,342, tops in the AFC), touchdowns (10) and punt returns (10.1-yard average) to earn a Pro Bowl spot for the fifth time in 1995.

*Sunrise warms the San Francisco Bay
as the Golden Gate Bridge snuggles
under a blanket of fog. The Bay Bridge,
just visible to the left, is spotlighted by a
ray of morning sunlight.*

Part Two

GOVERNMENT ADMINISTRATION

OFFICE OF THE MAYOR OF SAN FRANCISCO

If the Bay Area is California's crowning glory, then San Francisco is the brightest jewel in that crown. In 1995, Willie Lewis Brown Jr. was elected Mayor of the City and given the responsibility of making sure San Francisco does not lose its legendary sparkle.

Aside from the multifaceted, day-to-day duties involved in keeping the City running smoothly, one of the major concerns of Mayor Brown and his staff is the attraction, retention and marketing of businesses, both small and large.

Willie Lewis Brown Jr., Mayor of the City of San Francisco.

City of San Francisco; Photographer-Dennis De Silva

Believing that a business-friendly city is a city that can best respond to its citizens' many and varied needs, the Mayor's Office has set out to revitalize San Francisco's economy. In April of 1996, the Mayor convened the groundbreaking San Francisco Economic Summit, bringing together a variety of participants — including heads of major corporations, entrepreneurs, national and local labor leaders, federal officials, academics, economists, and concerned members of the City's neighborhoods — for two days of discussion centering upon San Francisco's economic future.

The resulting five-point action plan laid out the economic agenda of the Mayor's Office: first, to streamline the City's regulatory processes; second, to promote small businesses; third, to stimulate construction of affordable housing; fourth, to stimulate growth among current businesses and encourage new enterprises; and fifth, to coordinate job training and placement.

In its quest to reach these interconnected goals, the Mayor's Office utilizes many mechanisms — from traditional tools like fast-tracking the permit process and helping with project financing, to creating an Office of Economic Development and even participating in

projects like this one — to bring business to the City and the Bay Area.

The Mayor's Office has targeted emerging (and booming) Bay Area industries, including multimedia, biotechnology, financial services, and others, in an effort to foster the growth of new businesses and create job opportunities for Region.

By the year 2000, San Francisco will look very different. With the Mayor's office facilitating high-profile projects such as the redevelopment of the City's waterfront, the expansions of San Francisco International Airport and the Moscone Convention Center complex, and the erection of the Giants' new, privately financed Pacific Bell Baseball Park, the City should see itself in the midst of a continuing economic climb.

One would expect nothing less of the world-class City that serves as the economic, cultural and international trade hub of the Bay Area; a City that, over the years, has proven equally attractive to both artists and entrepreneurs.

Mayor's Office Of Housing

Senator Barbara Boxer, MOH Director Marcia Rosen, and Mayor Willie Brown on-site at 101 Valencia, a project which combined rehabilitation and new construction to transform a historic Salvation Army Building into affordable housing. Through measures such as Proposition A, Mayor Brown has advocated for affordable housing as a central component of urban economic development. As Chair of the United States Conference of Mayors' Housing Committee, Mayor Brown will bring San Francisco's excellence in housing policy to national prominence and will advocate for federal policies responsive to the needs of America's cities.

Like many affordable housing developments in San Francisco, Parkview Commons goes unnoticed by most visitors. However, to the 114 low- and moderate-income families who live in the development, Parkview Commons provides a rare opportunity to purchase a quality home at an affordable price in a city with one of the highest housing costs in the country. Using skilled architects and comprehensive community-based planning, Parkview Commons exemplifies the successful integration of affordable housing into the fabric of the surrounding neighborhood. The Mayor's Office of Housing (MOH) helped transform this site from an unused high school to a thriving residential community for first-time homebuyers by providing City funds for acquisition and development costs and ensuring the permanent affordability of units through its Resale Program. Parkview Commons is just one example of the high quality of affordable housing that is produced in San Francisco through careful attention to design and strong community involvement.

Safe and affordable housing provides the foundation upon which San Francisco's future as a vibrant world-class city will be built. The mission of the Mayor's Office of Housing is to coordinate the City's efforts to enhance affordable housing opportunities and, in doing so, preserve the vital economic and cultural mix that characterizes San Francisco. Utilizing innovative federal and local programs and working closely with financial institutions and developers to maximize available resources, MOH has been successful in funding the development of over 10,000 units of permanently affordable housing. MOH's programs have produced high-quality affordable rental units, expanded homeownership opportunities, improved safety and environmental conditions, and developed supportive housing for special needs communities throughout the City.

Mayor Brown recognizes the critical role that affordable housing plays in the ongoing economic development of San Francisco and exerts strong leadership in expanding affordable-housing options. He proposed an innovative affordable-housing bond measure (Proposition A) to generate $100 million of local funds to acquire, rehabilitate, and construct new rental housing units for low- and moderate-income San Franciscans and to assist first-time homebuyers. Supported by an historic coalition of political leaders, major banks and businesses, religious institutions, housing advocates, and community groups, Proposition A was approved by an overwhelming majority of San Francisco voters. MOH will continue to build lasting partnerships in order to provide housing options in San Francisco which keep pace with the City's economic growth and enrich the quality of life for the diverse communities that call San Francisco "home."

Parkview Commons, directly across the street from San Francisco's landmark Golden Gate Park, offers first time homeownership opportunities to low- and moderate- income families.

SAN FRANCISCO REDEVELOPMENT AGENCY

Situated on two blocks in San Francisco's "new" financial district, South of Market, the $330 million Moscone Convention Center occupies the blocks bounded by Mission, Folsom, Third and Fourth Streets. More than two-thirds of the City's 30,000 hotel rooms are within walking distance to the center.

The San Francisco Redevelopment Agency is the City's real estate investment arm. Using the unique powers of California Redevelopment Law, the Agency focuses public investments in blighted areas to attract private investment and improve living and working conditions in Redevelopment Project Areas and increase tax revenues to the City.

The Agency presently has eight active Project Areas under development. These include San Francisco's only business park,

India Basin Industrial Park, a new residential neighborhood, Rincon-Point South Beach, and Yerba Buena Center, a new neighborhood that includes San Francisco's Moscone Convention Center and the spectacular new Museum of Modern Art.

The Agency is preparing seven new Project Areas for intensive redevelopment. These areas include Mission Bay, two of San Francisco's closing naval bases, Treasure Island and Hunters Point Shipyard, and a new federal office building.

The Agency's investments include the areas of housing, economic development and quality of life. Over its forty-

year history, the Agency has facilitated the construction of more than 25,000 housing units, and has become the City's largest local provider of affordable housing. Its investment of public funds to promote economic development and improve the quality of life for San Francisco residents include parks and cultural/community facilities, as well as streets and other basic infrastructure.

SAN FRANCISCO POLICE DEPARTMENT

San Francisco has never lost its reputation as a place of opportunity combined with a high tolerance level that stems from its bohemian days of the last century. The City's sheer diversity, with people from virtually every country in the world, has encouraged an air of acceptance, and the fact that the City is geographically small — a mere 49 square miles — contributes to a sense of cohesion.

Under the leadership of Chief Fred Lau, the San Francisco Police Department mirrors the racial, ethnic and lifestyle diversity of the City's population, and also reflects the City's traditional tolerance for people, their ideas, their politics and their lifestyles. The

Fred H. Lau, San Francisco's 34th Chief of Police.

Department's 2,100 officers have a sense of proportion in their roles of keepers of the peace, knowing almost instinctively what constitutes a threat to the safety and well being of citizens and what does not. San Francisco police officers have a tradition of tempering their actions with restraint, maturity, and compassion. Far from being an occupation force, the members of the San Francisco Police Department constitute an integral part of the community. Officers are trained, not just in policing techniques, but also in the art of problem-solving, emphasizing friendliness and concern rather than intimidation and confrontation. The Department believes that its success is not measured by the number of arrests, but by the absence of crime.

The San Francisco Police Department is also an innovative department. It was one of the first police departments in the country to establish a mounted unit, a police academy, and continue in the forefront of such technological advancements as AFIS (Automated Fingerprint Indexing System). Recognizing the popularity of computers, and wanting to keep a constant open channel of communication, SFPD has established a computer web site for

SFPD bicycle patrol shares the road with a cable car.

citizens, particularly students, to discuss issues and to pose questions directly to the Chief.

SFPD is also encouraging citizens to become involved. The new Citizens' Academy introduces interested persons to the many aspects of policing. The Department is also one of the first to organize citizen patrols, where citizens walk their neighborhoods and work with officers to help improve neighborhood quality of life. All SFPD stations have community rooms where command staff regularly meet with neighborhood residents.

This spirit of community interaction, the diversity of its members and their recognition of a variety of values, combined with an emphasis on training and technological advancement, continue to ensure the uniqueness of the San Francisco Police Department.

KEY PLAYERS

Companies and organizations dedicated to making the Bay Area a better place to live, work and do business.

BANK OF CANTON OF CALIFORNIA
555 Montgomery Street
San Francisco, CA 94111
Phone: (415) 362-4100
Fax: (415) 989-0103
Page 116

CALIFORNIA STATE AUTOMOBILE
ASSOCIATION
100 Van Ness Avenue
San Francisco, CA 94102
Phone: (415) 565-2012
Web Site Address: www.csaa.com
Page 110

CITY COLLEGE OF SAN FRANCISCO
50 Phelan Avenue
San Francisco, CA 94112
Phone: (415) 239-3285
Fax: (415) 239-3918
Web Site Address:
http://hills.ccsf.cc.ca.us:9878/
Page 155

DEPARTMENT OF VETERANS AFFAIRS
MEDICAL CENTER, SAN FRANCISCO
4150 Clement St.
San Francisco, CA 94121
Phone: (415) 750-2250
Fax: (415) 750-2185
Web Site Address:
http://www.va.ucsf.edu/
Page 157

DES ARCHITECTS + ENGINEERS
399 Bradford St.
Redwood City, CA 94063
Phone: (415) 364-6453
Fax: (415) 364-2618
Page 124

EDEN MEDICAL CENTER
20103 Lake Chabot Road
Castro Valley, CA 94546
Phone: (510) 537-1234
Fax: (510) 889-6506
Page 150

ERNST & YOUNG LLP
555 California Street, Suite 1700
San Francisco, CA 94104
Phone: (415) 951-3000
Fax: (415) 421-8440
Web Site Address: http://ww.ey.com
Page 117

GENENTECH, INC.
460 Point San Bruno Blvd.
South San Francisco, CA 94080
Phone: (415) 225-2868
Fax: (415) 225-2021
Web Site Address:
http://www.gene.com
Page 130

INTEGRATED SYSTEMS, INC.
201 Moffett Park Drive
Sunnyvale, CA 94089
Phone: (408) 542-1500
Fax: (408) 542-1950
Web Site Address:
http://www.isi.com
Page 138

LAM RESEARCH CORPORATION
4650 Cushing Parkway
Fremont, CA 94538-6470
Phone: (510) 659-0200
Fax: (510) 572-2935
Web Site Address:
http://www.lamrc.com
Page 132

KKSF RADIO
455 Market Street, Suite 2300
San Francisco, CA 94105
Phone: (415) 975-5555
Fax: (415) 975-5573
Web Site Address:
http://www.kksf.com/kksf/
Page 96

THE MAYOR'S OFFICE
401 Van Ness Avenue
San Francisco, CA 94102
Phone: (415) 554-6141
Fax: (415) 554-6160
Web Site Address: www.ci.sf.ca.us.
Page 168

MAYOR'S OFFICE OF HOUSING
25 Van Ness Avenue, Suite 700
San Francisco, CA 94102
Phone: (415) 252-3177
Fax: (415) 252-3140
Page 169

METLIFE
2175 No. California Blvd.
Suite 610
Walnut Creek, CA 94596
Phone: (510) 946-0136
Fax: (510 946-0534
Web Site Address: www.metlife.com
Page 114

NEW UNITED MOTOR
MANUFACTURING, INC.
45500 Fremont Blvd.
Fremont, CA 94538
Phone: (510) 498-5763
Fax: (510) 770-4010
Page 144

OAKLAND RAIDERS
1220 Harbor Bay Parkway
Alameda, CA 94502
Phone: (510) 864-5000
Fax: (510) 864-5134
Web Site Address: raidersnet.com
Page 165

OLYMPIAN
260 Michelle Ct.
South San Francisco, CA 94080
Phone: (415) 873-8200
Fax: (415) 871-2264
Web Site Address: www.oly.com
Page 136

ORRICK, HERRINGTON &
SUTCLIFFE LLP
Old Federal Reserve Bank Building
400 Sansome Street
San Francisco, CA 94111-3143
Phone: (415) 392-1122
Fax: (415) 773-5759
Web Site Address: www.orrick.com
Page 106

PATSON DEVELOPMENT COMPANY
340 Pine Street
7th Floor Penthouse
San Francisco, CA 94104
Phone: (415) 788-2995
Fax: (415) 788-2326
Page 126

PCL CONSTRUCTION
SERVICES, INC.
200 Burchett Street
Glendale, CA 91203
Phone: (818) 246-3481
Fax: (818) 247-5775
Web Site Address:
http://www.pcl.ca
Page 122

PORT OF SAN FRANCISCO
The Ferry Building, Room 3100
San Francisco, CA 94111
Phone: (415) 274-0400
Fax: (415) 274-0528
Web Site Address: www.sfport.com
Page 98

SAN FRANCISCO BAY AREA RAPID
TRANSIT DISTRICT
800 Madison Street
Oakland, CA 94607
Phone: (510) 464-6000
Web Site Address:
http://www.bart.org
Page 100

SAN FRANCISCO BUSINESS TIMES
275 Battery Street, Suite 940
San Francisco, CA 94111
Phone: (415) 989-2522
Fax: (415) 398-2494
Web Site Address: http://www.amci-ty.com/sanfrancisco
Page 118

SAN FRANCISCO CONVENTION & VISITORS BUREAU
201 Third Street, Suite 900
San Francisco, CA 94103
Phone: (415) 974-6900
Fax: (415) 974-1992
Page 164

SAN FRANCISCO GIANTS
3 Com Park
San Francisco, CA 94124
Phone: (415) 468-3700
Fax: (415) 330-2725
Web Site Address:
http://www.sfgiants.com
Page 162

SAN FRANCISCO HILTON AND TOWERS
333 O'Farrell Street
San Francisco, CA 94102
Phone: (415) 771-1400
Fax: (415) 771-6807
Web Site Address:
http://www.hilton.com
Page 160

SAN FRANCISCO INTERNATIONAL AIRPORT
P.O. Box 8097
San Francisco, CA 94128
Phone: (415) 794-5000
Fax: (415) 794-5005
Page 92

SAN FRANCISCO MUNICIPAL RAILWAY
949 Presidio Avenue
San Francisco, CA 94115
Phone: (415) 923-6162
Fax: (415) 923-6166
Web Site Address:
http://www.ci.sf.ca.us/muni/
Page 103

SAN FRANCISCO POLICE DEPARTMENT
850 Bryant Street
San Francisco, CA 94103
Phone: (415) 553-1651
Fax: (415) 553-9229
Web Site Address:
http://www.ci.sf.ca.us:80/police/
Page 171

SAN FRANCISCO REDEVELOPMENT AGENCY
770 Golden Gate Avenue
San Francisco, CA 94102
Phone: (415) 749-2400
Fax: (415) 749-2565
Web Site Address:
http://www.ci.sf.ca.us/sfra//
Page 170

SANWA BANK CALIFORNIA
444 Market Street
San Francisco, CA 94111
Phone: (415) 597-5404
Fax: (415) 597-5408
Web Site Address:
www.sanwa-bank-ca.com
Page 119

SCICLONE PHARMACEUTICALS, INC.
901 Mariners Island Blvd.
San Mateo, CA 94404
Phone: (415) 358-3456
Fax: (415) 358-3469
Web Site Address: http://www.bio-space.com/sciclone
Page 134

SHAKLEE CORPORATION
444 Market Street
San Francisco, CA 94111
Phone: (415) 954-3000
Fax: (415) 954-2280
Web Site Address: www.shaklee.com
Page 152

SPRINT
1850 Gateway Drive
San Mateo, CA 94404
Phone: (415) 513-2000
Fax: (415) 513-2697
Web Site Address: www.sprint.com
Page 102

STANFORD UNIVERSITY
Stanford, CA 94305
Phone: (415) 723-2300
Web Site Address:
http://www.stanford.edu
Page 156

TCSI CORPORATION
1080 Marina Village Parkway
Alameda, CA 94501-1046
Phone: (510) 649-3700
Fax: (510) 649-3500
Web Site Address: www.tcsi.com
Page 133

UNIVERSITY OF CALIFORNIA SAN FRANCISCO
3333 California Street, Suite 103
San Francisco, CA 94143-0462
Phone: (415) 476-2557
Fax: (415) 476-3541
Web Site Address:
http://www.ucsf.edu
Page 154

USS-POSCO INDUSTRIES
P.O. Box 471
Pittsburg, CA 94565
Phone: (510) 439-6000
Fax: (510) 439-6506
Page 142

WASHINGTON HOSPITAL HEALTHCARE SYSTEM
2000 Mowry Avenue
Fremont, CA 94538
Phone: (510) 791-3417
Fax: (510) 745-6427
Page 148

THE WINE ALLIANCE
132 Mill Street
Healdsburg, CA 95448
Phone: (707) 433-8268
Fax: (707) 433-3538
Page 145

BIBLIOGRAPHY

BEARSS, EDWIN C.
Redwood National Park, del Norte and Humboldt Counties
U.S. Dept. of the Interior, Washington D.C. 1982

BOLTON, HERBERT EUGENE
Anza's California Expeditions
University of California Press, Berkeley, CA 1930

BOLTON, HERBERT EUGENE
Outpost of Empire
Alfred A. Knopf, New York 1931

BRONSON, WILLIAM
The Earth Shook, The Sky Burned
Doubleday, Garden City, NY 1959

BRUCE, CURT
The Great Houses of San Francisco
Alfred A. Knopf, New York 1974

CAMP, WILLIAM MARTIN
San Francisco: Port of Gold
Doubleday, Garden City, NY 1947

CHINN, THOMAS W.
Bridging the Pacific: San Francisco's Chinatown and its people
Chinese Historical Society of America, San Francisco 1989

CHIRICH, NANCY, WITH SIMPKINS, JOHN
Life With Wine: A Self-Portrait of the Wine Business in the Napa and Sonoma Valleys
Ed-it Productions, Oakland 1984

COLE, TOM
A Short History of San Francisco
Don't Call It Frisco Press
San Francisco 1989

COLLIER'S ENCYCLOPEDIA

COMPTON'S LIVING RNCYCLOPEDIA

CONAWAY, JAMES
Napa
Houghton Mifflin, Boston 1990

COSTANSO, MIGUEL
Noticias of the Port of San Francisco ... in the year 1772
Windsor Press, San Francisco, CA 1940

COSTANSO, MIGUEL
The Discovery of San Francisco Bay: The Portola Expedition of 1769-1770
Great West Books, Lafayette, CA 1992

DOHERTY, CRAIG A. AND KATHERINE M.
The Golden Gate Bridge
Blackbirch Press, Woodbridge, CN 1995

EAGLE, ADAM FORTUNATE
Alcatraz, Alcatraz! The Indian Occupation of 1969-1971
Heydey Books, Berkeley 1992

ENCYCLOPEDIA BRITTANNICA

FREUDENHEIM, LESLIE MANDELSON
Building with Nature: Roots of the San Francisco Bay Region Tradition
P. Smith, Santa Barbara, CA 1974

GROLIER'S MULTIMEDIA ENCYCLOPEDIA

HANNA, WARREN LEONARD
Lost Harbor: The Controversy Over Drake's California Anchorage
University of California Press, Berkeley 1979

KENNEDY, JOHN CASTILLO
The Great Earthquake and Fire, San Francisco 1906
Morrow, New York 1963

LEMKE, NANCY
Cabrillo: First European Explorer of the California Coast
EZ Nature Books, San Luis Obispo, CA 1991

LEWIS, OSCAR
San Francisco: Mission to Metropolis
Howell-North Books, Berkeley 1966

LOTCHIN, ROGER W.
San Francisco 1846-1856: from Hamlet to City
Oxford University Press, New York, 1974

MCDOUGALL, RUTH BRANSTEN
Coffee, Martinis, and San Francisco
Presidio Press, San Rafael, CA 1978

O'BRIEN, ROBERT
This is San Francisco: A Classic Portrait of the City
Chronicle Books, San Francisco, CA 1994

POMADA, ELIZABETH
The Painted Ladies Revisited
Dutton, New York 1989

QUILLEN, JIM
Alcatraz From Inside: The Hard Years, 1942-52
Golden Gate National Park Association, San Francisco 1991

REISENBERG, FELIX
Golden Gate: the Story of San Francisco Harbor
Alfred A. Knopf, New York, London 1949

SAN FRANCISCO ECONOMIC DEVELOPMENT CORPORATON
Smart Land Heart Land: A Book About The San Francisco Bay Area
SFEDC 1991

STEWART, GEORGE RIPPEY
Committee of Vigilance: Revolution in San Francisco, 1851
Houghton Mifflin, Boston, MS 1964

WATKINS, TOM H.
Mirror of the Dream: An Illustrated History of San Francisco
Scrimshaw Press, San Francisco 1976

WHITE, STEWART EDWARD
Old California in Picture and Story
Doubleday, Doran, Garden City, NY 1937

INDEX